INSPIRED *by* NATURE

THE GARFIELD PARK CONSERVATORY AND CHICAGO'S WEST SIDE

⸻⸻⸻⸻⸻ ✦ ⸻⸻⸻⸻⸻

BY JULIA S. BACHRACH AND JO ANN NATHAN
WITH A FOREWORD BY ALEX KOTLOWITZ
AND CONTEMPORARY PHOTOGRAPHY BY BROOK COLLINS

PUBLISHED BY THE GARFIELD PARK CONSERVATORY ALLIANCE
IN ASSOCIATION WITH THE CHICAGO PARK DISTRICT

PUBLISHER'S NOTES

Front cover photo: Garfield Park Conservatory, ca. 1930; Chicago Park District Special Collections.

Back cover photo: Students examining plants, 2002; Brook Collins, Chicago Park District.

Flap photo: Authors, from left to right, Julia S. Bachrach and Jo Ann Nathan, 2007; Brook Collins, Chicago Park District.

Many of the photographs were cropped to accommodate the book's trim size. For illustration credits, see page 146.

Designed and typeset by Jell Creative, Inc., Chicago, Illinois.

Printed in Canada by Friesens Corporation.

Distributed by the University of Chicago Press
1427 East 60th Street
Chicago, Illinois 60637-2954

The Garfield Park Conservatory Alliance has published this book with the generous support of:

 Lead Sponsor:
Chicago Park District

 Lead Corporate Sponsor:
Sara Lee Foundation

Additional support provided by:
Chicago Public Schools
The Richard H. Driehaus Foundation
Parkways Foundation

 Garfield Park Conservatory Alliance
300 North Central Park Avenue
Chicago, Illinois 60624
www.garfieldconservatory.org

ISBN: 978-0-9794125-0-9
(ISBN-10: 0-9794125-0-1)

Acknowledgements

This project has been an extremely enriching experience for both of us, heightened by the many supportive organizations and talented individuals who have helped us bring *Inspired by Nature: The Garfield Park Conservatory and Chicago's West Side* to life. In 2006, Michael W. Scott, former president of both the Chicago Park District Board of Commissioners and the Chicago Public School Board, envisioned a book to honor the 100th anniversary of the iconic Garfield Park Conservatory. His involvement has made this project possible. The Garfield Park Conservatory Alliance stretched its mission to become a publisher. We thank Chairman Tony Hernandez, the Board of the Alliance, President Eunita Rushing, and staff members Sandra Wilcoxon, Mike Tomas, and Rishona Taylor, as well as the delightful Green Teens who gave valuable insights.

We are very grateful for the commitment of the Chicago Park District, especially General Superintendent Timothy J. Mitchell. Along with the essential role of photojournalist Brook Collins, other staff members gave us meaningful input including Gia Biagi, Adam Schwerner, Mary Eysenbach, Art Richardson, Jessica Maxey-Faulkner, John Raffetto, Steve Meyer, Erin Swanborn, and interns Elizabeth Frantz, Nidhi Goyal, Emily Ruzzo, and Natalia Salazar. Several colleagues previously with the Park District who provided valuable assistance include Arnold Randall, Lisa Roberts, Ed Uhlir, David Alvarez, and Dan Purciarello. We also thank the Parkways Foundation for commissioning Alex Kotlowitz to write the foreword.

We appreciate Rachel Moore who helped with interviews, and the former and current West Siders who shared their memories: Vincent Alloco, Demetrius Armstrong, Zelda Bachrach, Nettie Bailey, Beverly Chubat, George Cotsirilos, Irving Cutler, Diane Kelley, Mary Nelson, Mattie Simpson, Mello Sam, Reverend Eudora Ramey, Mike and Marley Sackheim, Bernard Sahlins, Jean Sanno, Mary Scott-Boria, and Edna Stewart. Willa Cather Elementary School students also provided their reflections, and special thanks go to Lynnto Craig and the wonderful teaching staff.

We are grateful to Tim Samuelson and Vince Michael for their historical input, and Rob Medina, Bruce Moffat, Michael Steiber, and Teresa Yoder for access to archival images. We appreciate Marta Juaniza and Zvezdana Kubat of the Chicago Park District Press Office, as well as Jill Riddell and Stephanie Yiu for copy-editing. Most importantly, our heartfelt thanks go to Joe Grossmann, Veronica Bardauskis, Wailam Pan, Shayla Johnson, Ty Cooper, and Tricia Kazmar of Jell Creative — an extraordinary team that exceeded all of our expectations.

—*Julia S. Bachrach and Jo Ann Nathan*

Contents

FOREWORD

by Alex Kotlowitz

On a recent summer afternoon, I went for a walk in Garfield Park with my nine-year-old son, Lucas. The mercury hovered around ninety, the humidity so thick the foliage was sweating. Just south of the Conservatory, which is known in the neighborhood as "the Flower House," we stopped to watch receivers and defensive backs from the Al Raby High School football team run passing drills. The school doesn't have a football field so it uses the park as its practice facility, as do two other West Side schools, Crane and Providence St.-Mel. We visited with a few of the fishermen who, at the edge of one of the two lagoons, sat on crates and chairs, their bobbers disappointingly inactive. One of the men, Dale, who looked to be in his forties, had smoked his Newport down to a nub, and as he flicked it to the ground, told us that he'd brought his wife out here but "she was ready to go in ten minutes so I told her I got a solution: Come here by myself." He offered to sell us a rod and reel for ten dollars, but we declined.

Garfield Park is a community prairie, a luscious open expanse nearly the size of the Brookfield Zoo which sometimes plays second fiddle to the Conservatory, but in fact is what the neighbors take most pride in. On summer afternoons at the lagoons you can enjoy the sight of children sailing, or in the Gold Dome watch children dancing in the Alvin Ailey camp or boxing under the guidance of George Hernandez whose fighters have gone onto the Olympics and the pro ranks. Indeed, as we continued our stroll, two amateur boxers in heavy sweats running laps waved to us. Farther south, a Hispanic man who cares for the twelve carefully arranged flower beds was planting marigolds; he told us that already this year he had to replace sixty-five plants because local residents regularly dig them up for their own backyards which, all things considered, doesn't seem like such a bad thing. A way of sharing nature, I suppose. And finally at the Music Court, which is known as the circle, we chatted with a group of a dozen older men, all part of a CB club, their cars parked nearby with six-foot antennas spiraling above them. The men sat in the shade of the park's old band shell. The men introduced themselves to us by their handles—Chastising, Pathfinder, and Shaggy Dog. The latter, a beer-bellied man with a droopy mustache, seemed well-suited to his name. As we walked on, my son turned around, and said, "See y'a later, Shaggy Dog." They all laughed in unison, and urged us to stop by again.

Opposite page: Fishing in Garfield Park's lagoon west of Gold Dome building, 2007.
Previous page: City Garden and Garfield Park Conservatory, 2007.

Open space is wonderful, especially in crowded cities. But what's become clear over time is that open space alone is not enough. It's how it's used. Who it attracts. Where it's placed. What's so remarkable about Garfield Park is that it sits smack in the middle of Chicago's West Side. You can't avoid it. Five major roads slice through it or skirt it. The "L" runs along its northern border. To the west is the West Side's main shopping district, a string of clothing and discount stores. To the east are a number of high schools. Greystones and apartment buildings ring the park like soldiers standing guard. There is life in the communities adjacent to the park—and so it remains to reason there is life, abundant life, inside it, as well.

In the 1960s, the complexion of much of the West Side changed virtually overnight, from white to black, and of course as we now know this was not by accident. In the summer of 1966 Martin Luther King, Jr. moved into an apartment here to fight for open housing in the city, and then when he was later killed in Memphis, residents in their grief and anger took to the streets, burning much of Madison Street, the West Side's commercial boulevard. It is common wisdom that the West Side never recovered from that devastation, but truth be told, life here was hard and gritty before, and so the riots didn't mark some magical moment when all went downhill. Things were sliding long before.

The West Side still struggles though some things are looking up. New homes have sprouted. Schools have been repaired. There's a pride about living here; a number of years ago the youth here began to wear hats which read simply *West Side*, as if it didn't need any explaining. And if Garfield Park is any barometer, there is reason for more hope.

Often parks lag behind a community's revival. They're an afterthought, an adjective easily disposed of. But here the conservatory and Garfield Park have become the community's heart, its lifeblood. There is a sense at Garfield Park, given its size, that you can push some of those daily pressures away for a bit. That you can hide from that which pulls at you. That you can unwind. That you can find companionship. Years ago, when I was spending virtually everyday at the Henry Horner Homes, a West Side public housing complex which no longer exists, I would usually find myself on the front stoop talking with the adults, or in the playground playing a makeshift game of basketball (the kids used the jungle gym as a hoop), or crouching beneath a tree for shade. Unlike Garfield Park, there was nothing green about this courtyard, but it was an open space, a place where people gathered, where they felt secure, where they found companionship. Garfield Park is that writ large—and with an elegant beauty about it. It should come as no surprise that while parts of the West Side are plagued by crime, there is little in Garfield Park. The park has a seductive quality about it. At one point my son and I got turned around between the two lagoons, and, as if we were in the north woods, momentarily lost a sense of where we were. (Some young boys, fresh from a dip in the park's swimming pool, pointed us in the right direction.) What's more, the conservatory attracts outsiders to the neighborhood, people who otherwise might never set foot on the West Side. At Edna's, a local soul food restaurant, much of its clientele on weekends are white Americans and Europeans visiting the flower house.

This book is a celebration of Garfield Park and the conservatory—and by extension a celebration of the West Side. The history and the soul of this community can be found within the boundaries of this vast open space. It is a place as lively as it is lovely.

As my son and I finished our walk just south of the Conservatory, we stopped briefly to shoot baskets with a 58-year-old postman who had a day off. In sandals, he was unfurling jump shots, compensating for the breeze that blew off the lagoon. He asked me my age, and when I told him, he invited me to his early Sunday morning games for old-timers like ourselves. I told him I'd be back out, and as Lucas and I headed to our car, we made one last stop at Red Boyz, an open grill where a middle-aged man had just put on a fresh batch of turkey legs and polish sausages. They weren't quite cooked yet so we bought a pop and bottle of water. "Happy late Father's Day," the concessionaire offered. "Come on back." We will.

Alex Kotlowitz is the author of *There Are No Children Here: The Story of Two Boys Growing Up in the Other America* (1992), *The Other Side of the River: A Story of Two Towns, a Death and America's Dilemma* (1998), and *Never a City So Real* (2004). He is the recipient of the Helen B. Bernstein Award for Excellence in Journalism, the Carl Sandburg Award, and a Christopher Award. The New York Public Library selected *There Are No Children Here* as one of the 150 most important books of the century.

LOCATED FIVE MILES WEST OF DOWNTOWN, Garfield Park is an intriguing green space amidst the urban grid. This verdant tapestry of lagoons, landscapes, diverse architecture, and sculptures represents many layers of history and the work of several talents. Chicago's early park proponents and designers recognized the value of nature in the city and have bequeathed us a living landmark.

Opposite page: Aerial view of Garfield Park looking south, 1941.

EARLY PARKS MOVEMENT

During the 1830s, Chicago's nascent government adopted the motto "Urbs en Horto," a Latin phrase meaning "City in a Garden." At the time, however, the young city of approximately four thousand residents had few parks.

Twenty years later, amidst a flurry of real estate speculation, citizens asked the City of Chicago to create green spaces similar to the Boston Commons. One park advocate urged:

> "Our wives and children are feeling seriously the want of a place for promenade, where they can get needful exercise and enjoy pure air without the thousand annoyances now experienced. We shall never have a better opportunity than now to secure these blessings to our growing community. Real estate is on the market and can be bought at comparatively low prices."[1]

In 1853, West Side residents became especially alarmed when they saw a surveying party preparing to develop the area around West Lake and North Ashland streets. These neighbors convinced the speculators to sell some of the property to the City at a reduced price having argued that a public park would boost the value of the surrounding community.

Union Park, 1878. Along with an observation tower, the park had iron bridges, rustic benches, and a small zoo.

Jefferson Park, ca. 1875. This picturesque park remained unchanged until the 1950s, when the pond was filled to make way for ball fields and the site was renamed Skinner Park.

After naming it Union Park in honor of the Federal Union, the City of Chicago completely ignored the site. Citizens complained that the small park was an eyesore until a decade later when the City finally transformed it into a whimsical fantasyland. Visitors watched swans and ducks floating gracefully on a large artificial lake from a nearby castle-like tower. Mayor Carter Harrison, a resident, described his neighbors parading "…in fine array, some driving slowly in wide open landaus, the populace looking on in rapt admiration." Comparing the park with a famous landscape in France, he added, "Union Park was the Bois de Boulogne of the West Side."[2]

Union Park and the only other West Side green space, Jefferson Park, attracted wealthy Chicagoans to settle in the neighborhood. Jefferson Park (now Skinner Park) was a back-drop for Theodore Dreiser's novel, *Sister Carrie*. In it, he described the park's little pond, where "…some cleanly dressed children were sailing white canvas boats. In the shade of a green pagoda a be-buttoned officer of the law was resting, his arms folded, his club at rest in his belt."[3] But the two small fashionable parks were soon inadequate for the area's growing population.

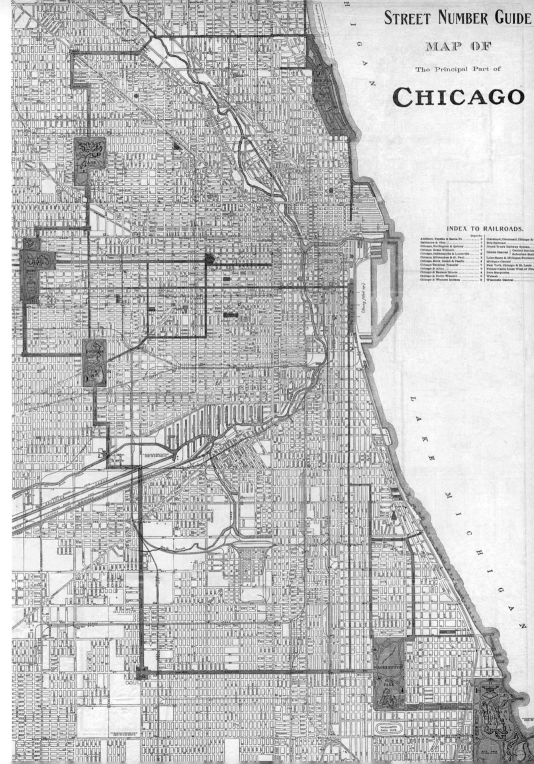

Left: Garfield Park's unimproved site, ca. 1870.
Right: Rand Mc Nally & Co. Street Number Guide, 1902.
This map shows Chicago's park and boulevard system.

CIRCLE OF GREEN

Chicagoans pressed for a more ambitious system of parks. This movement resulted in three separate acts of state legislation in 1869 establishing the Lincoln, South, and West Park Commissions. Although they operated independently, the goal was to create a continuous ribbon of green that would encircle the city.

This proved to be the first comprehensive park and boulevard system in America. The city's early park proponents, according to historian Ted Turak:

> "…intended to give Chicago what no American city yet had — a planned park system integrated into the urban fabric. Even Olmsted's great Central Park in New York remained aesthetically apart. It was inserted into the grid pattern of streets and stands in splendid, rectangular isolation to its environment… Chicago planners, on the other hand, saw parks in series forming a green belt around the city."[4]

The centerpiece of the West Park System was 185-acre Central Park, now known as Garfield Park. Tree-lined boulevards would link it to Humboldt Park on the north and Douglas Park on the south. William Le Baron Jenney created the original plans for the entire West Park System.

WILLIAM LE BARON JENNEY

An architect, engineer, and landscape architect, William Le Baron Jenney (1832–1907) had an impressive background. Born into a prosperous New England family, he began studying engineering at Harvard University but was dissatisfied with the curriculum. He moved to Paris to attend the rigorous and highly-respected L'Ecole Centrale des Arts et Manufactures. After finishing his studies, he worked as an engineer, first in Mexico and then back in Paris for the Bureau of American Securities, a firm that encouraged Europeans to invest in American railroads.

At the outbreak of the Civil War, the company's president, William Tecumseh Sherman, convinced the young engineer to join the Union Army. Jenney was assigned engineering duties under Generals Grant and Sherman. At Vicksburg, Jenney met Frederick Law Olmsted (1822–1903), who was there as a member of the United States Sanitary Commission. Only a few years earlier, Olmsted, the nation's most famous landscape architect, had created New York City's Central Park. The meeting between the affable young Jenney and the influential landscape designer marked the beginning of a lifelong friendship.

At the end of the Civil War, Jenney wrote to Olmsted expressing his ambitions as a designer, stating:

> "There is no situation that I can imagine when I should derive more pleasure from the work I might be called upon to perform as one in which Architecture, Gardening and Engineering were associated and I most earnestly desire and hope that some such position be within my reach." [5]

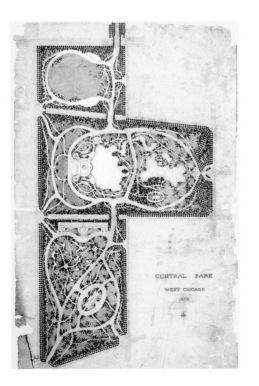

Central Park Plan, 1870. This is William Le Baron Jenney's original plan for Garfield Park.

In 1868, Olmsted and his partner, Calvert Vaux designed Riverside, Illinois, the first planned community in the United States. Olmsted hired Jenney, who had recently settled in Chicago, as the architect for buildings in Riverside and to supervise the implementation of its landscape.

Some of Chicago's prominent citizens had hoped that Olmsted would design the entire system of parks and boulevards. [6] Only the South Park Commission, however, could afford the renowned firm of Olmsted & Vaux. The West Park Commissioners turned to a more affordable alternative, Olmsted's friend and colleague, William Le Baron Jenney.

CHICAGO'S CENTRAL PARK

The unimproved west park sites were flat, swampy, and dreary. Central Park proved to be the most challenging of the three. Jenney had to transform "a flat, naked, cold and undrained prairie of clay, destitute of any natural beauty" into verdant landscape. [7]

The T-shaped site was divided into three parts by existing roadways. Jenney planned to conceal them through grading and planting techniques. Poor soil conditions required that large quantities of compost be added before any plants could grow. He addressed the property's drainage problems by designing two artificial lakes in the center of the park connected by a serpentine stream. Bridges would extend over the stream. A large picturesque bandstand and terrace, a rustic playhouse, and monumental tower were also planned for this area.

With the park's northern landscape rendered as a pastoral meadow, Jenney wanted the southern area to focus on natural history with a museum and a conservatory. This area would also have a zoo, botanic gardens, deer paddock, and farm animals. He wrote:

"It would be interesting to our farmers, and country gentlemen to see pure specimens of the finest breeds of cattle and sheep. A place should be provided for them to range, with a dairy house where milk can be sold and drank." [8]

Jenney designed several formal entryways into this area with fanciful names such as the "Herdsman Gate," the "Farmers Gate," and "Audubon Gate." [9]

EARLIEST PARK IMPROVEMENTS

Although Jenney had a grand vision for the challenging site, the West Park Commissioners did not have enough money to build the entire park all at once. He suggested initially improving the easternmost forty acres between West Lake and West Madison streets. Because of the park's significance to the system and its difficult natural site, this improvement was considered the "first battle ground." [10] Jenney believed that with just a "moderate expenditure," the public could see "what may be hoped for from even a prairie park." [11]

Dredging, grading, and construction began in 1871. Two years later, laborers planted more than a thousand trees and shrubs. The work in this forty-acre area closely followed Jenney's plan, with two islands, boat landings, and a suspension bridge. An elliptical entryway at West Washington Boulevard was the only one of Jenney's formal gateways implemented.

Throngs of exuberant people gathered in the park for its official opening in August of 1874. A newspaper article lauded the "handsome acres reclaimed from the desolate prairie." [12]

Left: Central Park's lagoon, 1872.
Right: Washington Boulevard entrance, 1872.
These photographs show Garfield Park's earliest improvements. The sign in the right hand photograph says "Please keep off the finished ground."

Left: Central Park's Bird Island, 1875. Right: Boaters near suspension bridge in Central Park, 1875.

THE PLEASING RESORT

Satisfied that the forty acres had become a "pleasing resort," Jenney shifted his role in 1875 to consulting architect and engineer for just one year, but was later hired to design individual park structures.[13] His work for the West Park System led to commissions for other Illinois landscapes such as the Willowmere extension to Chicago's Graceland Cemetery, Riverside Cemetery in Moline, and Lake Forest Cemetery.

Jenney's office was the training ground for important figures including Louis Sullivan, Daniel H. Burnham and landscape gardener Ossian Cole Simonds, who had studied under Jenney at the University of Michigan. His greatest fame would come from architecture with the developments he made to the skeletal steel frame which garnered him the moniker "father of the skyscraper." His accomplishments as a landscape designer were so completely overlooked, that they were not even mentioned in his obituaries.

CENTRAL PARK BECOMES GARFIELD PARK

Surrounded by unpaved muddy streets, Central Park was an attractive anomaly on Chicago's West Side. The picturesque setting drew large crowds especially in the summertime. Boats placed on the park's lagoon attracted nearly 10,000 patrons annually. Because of Central Park's prominence, a barrage of newspaper articles and letters suggested that it should be renamed in honor of President James A. Garfield following his assassination. Within a month of the president's death in September of 1881, the West Park Commissioners formally renamed the grounds as Garfield Park.

IMPROVEMENTS BY OSCAR F. DUBUIS

In the early 1880s, the West Park System's new engineer, Oscar F. Dubuis (1849–1906) began focusing on unimproved areas in Garfield Park. Born in Switzerland, Dubuis had studied at Polytechnic Institute at Winterthur and apprenticed for a Swiss architect. After settling in Chicago in 1870, he began working for Jenney, eventually succeeding him.

Carrying out Jenney's overall intent for Garfield Park, Dubuis extended the lagoon to the west, created a peninsula, and installed a rockery at the artesian well that fed the lagoon. Renowned architect John Welborn Root designed a refectory building—a park pavilion overlooking the water.

It was important to Dubuis to create attractive landscape scenery. His waterway, meant to emulate a "forest stream," had an irregular shape with "numerous small rapids and eddies among rocks and ferns."[14] Although he did not revere the native Midwestern landscape, Dubuis was concerned about designing features that would be appropriate to the area's natural characteristics. Warning against creating any dramatic hills in Garfield Park, he suggested that "…it is obviously impossible to produce in the vicinity of Chicago such scenery as will affect the mind as it is affected by mountain scenery."[15] In the same spirit, he suggested planting masses of wild shrubbery near Garfield Park's lagoon.

Dubuis served as the West Park System's engineer until 1893. He then worked briefly for the Lincoln Park Commission, and went on to spend the remainder of his life designing and managing the parks and boulevards of Peoria, Illinois.

West lagoon in Garfield Park, 1888. John Welborn Root's Queen Anne-style refectory is the prominent structure on the opposite side of the lagoon.

FASCINATION WITH THE EXOTIC

Between the 1880s and 1890s, a widespread interest in exotic plants and forms influenced the development of Garfield Park. The West Park Commissioners replaced a small hothouse with a more impressive conservatory that had public display houses in 1888. Surrounded by lush gardens, the wood and glass building was located on the west side of Garfield Park near South Hamlin Avenue.

West Park gardeners created showy floral displays during the 1890s. Many followed the popular Victorian practice of "carpet bedding" in which fanciful patterns were created out of foliage. One example spelled out Garfield Park's name. Another emulated Fort Dearborn, Chicago's historic federal military installation, while a third provided a "peristyle" gateway into the park.

A taste for the exotic was also expressed in the architecture of the period. A Jenney-designed Chinese pagoda sheathed what would have been a mundane electrical station and water tower. In the late 1890s, architect Joseph Lyman Silsbee designed a French Gothic bridge and Flemish Revival style power house. Silsbee's fanciful bandstand, made of marble and glass mosaic, "...resembles in some respects the Indian architecture of the Saracenic type."[16]

Left: Pagoda-style water tower, 1897.
Right: Peristyle in Garfield Park, 1896. Surrounded by geometric beds of flowers, the "peristyle" gateway was a floral construction.

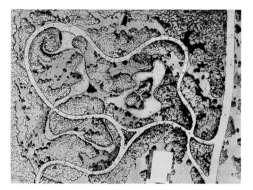

RECOMMENDING NATURAL SCENERY

Despite the popularity of Victorian gardens and exotic architecture, there was a burgeoning interest in naturalistic landscape designs. In the 1880s, West Park Commissioner Judge C.C. Kohlsaat (1844–1914) presented a plan to plant the area north of West Lake Street "with every variety of tree grown wild in this latitude."[17] Though it was approved, the board did not fund the work. Within a few years, an irregularly shaped stream designed by Dubuis was completed in that area. Judge Kohlsaat pressed for his naturalistic concept in 1897. He suggested that the indigenous forests at the outskirts of the city could serve as a model for his "wildwood" scheme. He wanted to people to fish and hunt in this "natural-looking" area of the park.

Kohlsaat's project was never realized, but Garfield Park's north stream became a popular spot for fly casting. At the turn of the century, the Chicago Fly Casting Club held its annual tournament there. A contest for distance and accuracy, the event did not really involve catching fish.

Kohlsaat and Dubuis were not alone in their interest in native trees, shrubs, and flowers. Jens Jensen, who began his career as a West Parks laborer, was the strongest proponent of this approach. While Kohlsaat and Dubuis contributed to the early context for naturalism in the west parks, Jensen went on to develop a cohesive design expression celebrating the native landscape. A tall red-headed man with a bushy mustache, Jensen was a commanding figure. He passionately believed in saving natural scenery from destruction, and when he spoke on the subject, his voice would often "screech like an eagle."[18] Today, Jensen is recognized as dean of the Prairie style in landscape architecture and leader of the conservation movement in the Midwest.

JENS JENSEN: LABORER ON THE RISE

Born in the Slesvig region of Denmark, Jens Jensen (1860–1951) spent much of his childhood outdoors enjoying nature. He had strong ties to his homeland, but when his class-conscious parents did not approve of his fiancée, Anne Marie Hansen, the young couple ran away to America. They settled in Chicago where Jensen found employment in 1885 as a day laborer for the West Park Commission. This low-level job proved to be the beginning of a remarkable career.

After a short time, Jensen was promoted to the position of gardener. Noting that exotic flowers—so popular at the time—didn't thrive well in Chicago, he said, "There's something wrong here. We are trying to force plants to grow where they don't want to grow."[19] In 1888, he embarked upon an experiment when he and his crew gathered wildflowers and transplanted them in Union Park. "We couldn't get the stock from nurserymen, as there had never been any requests for it, and we went out into the woods with a team and wagon and carted it in ourselves."[20] Although native plants were generally considered weeds, Jensen's innovative "American Garden" became extremely popular.

Rising through the ranks, Jensen became superintendent of Union Park in 1894, and by the end of the following year, superintendent of the larger, more prominent Humboldt Park. He soon received accolades for inventing special equipment for removing aquatic weeds. The weeds in Garfield Park's lagoon had become so abundant that they were interfering with boating. Jensen's "discovery was hailed with delight by the patrons of the lakes."[21]

VICTORIAN ACTIVITIES AND ATTRACTIONS

By the mid-1890s, Chicagoans were increasingly interested in a range of activities in the parks. Boating was a favorite pastime in Garfield Park, and its lagoon was stocked with bass, perch, and sun-fish so that boaters with proper permits could take advantage of fishing. The West Park Police had to contend with rampant poaching which often happened late at night. Poachers were only interested in catching bass. The other fish were not valuable enough to sell.

Other, more respectable activities had become popular. People frequented the park's green spaces for lawn tennis, football, croquet, and picnicking. As the German Turnverein movement caught on in Chicago, there were many organizations promoting physical and mental health through exercise. The West Park Commissioners set aside an area of Garfield Park for an open-air gymnasium in 1896. Five hundred male and female "Turners" gave gymnastics demonstrations at the dedication ceremonies. An audience of thousands witnessed "…the captivating picture of good health presented by the Turners." [22]

Bicycling had become the rage throughout America after the invention of the safety bike around 1885. Dozens of Chicago "wheelmen clubs" soon formed and cycling enthusiasts often raced along the boulevards and into Garfield Park. West Side club members began discussing the need for a bicycle track in the park in the early 1890s. This would provide a safer alternative to road racing or "scorching" which was dangerous and destructive to the pedestrians and horses on the roads. The commissioners agreed to build a double-ring track for horse and bicycle racing as part of an improvement project in the park south of West Madison Street.

Considering that a large horse racing facility already existed in the neighborhood just west of Garfield Park, it seems odd that the commissioners installed one within its boundaries. Years earlier, they had allowed the Gentleman's Trotting and Racing Club, also called the West Side Club, to encroach on the park with some stables and sheds. With the nearby race track came serious problems. The park became infested with illegal gambling and violent crimes such as the murder of a policeman.[23] There were many complaints about the "characters of unsavory reputation who congregate there, using loud and profane language." [24] Nearby residents requested that the club's stables and sheds be removed from the park and replaced with baseball fields. Ironically, the commissioners razed the structures and then built the new race track in that very location. Completed in 1896, the track had rings for horse and bicycle racing. In response to the neighbors' request, the interior oval lawn provided a field for baseball, football, and cricket.

Opposite page: Garfield Park bicycle and horse race track, 1899. This page: Two boys riding bicycles in Garfield Park, 1897.

CORRUPTION AND REFORM

By the late 1890s, the West Park Commission had become crippled by political corruption. Board members had spent hundreds of thousands of dollars on "…fraudulent lists of useless or superfluous employees."[25] In 1900, the park commissioners dismissed Jens Jensen for refusing to participate in schemes of graft. He then turned to private practice, working on the estates of a few affluent clients.

Five years later, reform-minded Governor Charles S. Deneen swept the entire board clean. In forming a new and progressive commission, he selected philanthropist and attorney, Bernard Eckhart as its president. Eckhart described the "deplorable conditions" that his board inherited:

> "…financially bankrupt, credit gone, boulevards impassable, sidewalks broken and out of grade, lawn spaces and park lawns exhausted, trees dead and dying, shrubbery destroyed, buildings all over the system tumbling down, scarcely any implements or tools available."[26]

Recognizing Jens Jensen as uniquely qualified to restore and properly manage the parks, the board created a new position for him. They appointed Jensen as General Superintendent and Chief Landscape Architect for the entire West Park System. A two-million dollar bond issue funded desperately needed repairs and improvements. These projects gave Jensen an opportunity to experiment with his evolving Prairie style.

Left: Unimproved area in Garfield Park, ca. 1905.
Right: Laborer with horse and wagon during landscape improvements, ca. 1907.

PRAIRIE-INSPIRED IMPROVEMENTS

After years of use and little maintenance, the finished landscapes in Humboldt, Garfield, and Douglas parks had suffered great damage. Jensen said the need to replant gave him the "opportunity of trying out on a large scale this idea of employing indigenous stock."[27] He also planted native vegetation in unfinished areas of each the parks that had been left as patches of weeds and vast expanses of mud. He planted lush native vegetation in unfinished areas of each of the parks, transforming unkempt patches of weed and expanses of mud into impressive naturalistic landscapes.

Horizontal meadows edged with masses of native trees and shrubs offered broad views and space for lawn tennis, baseball, and festivals. In Garfield Park, Jensen replaced the horse racing track with an extensive meadow. A metaphor for the prairie, this meadow served as the first public golf course on Chicago's West Side. A famous golf course designer, Tom Bendelow, helped Jensen minimize the visual impact of the required fairways and greens. An elegant Prairie-style golf shelter was built at the north end of the course.

Jensen made other improvements. He tore down the system's three small dilapidated greenhouses. After filling in the lagoon north of West Lake Street, he built the new centralized Garfield Park Conservatory there. Even though this structure would house tropical plants, Jensen used its design to continue exploring his ideas, using natural-looking water and stonework, planting directly into the ground, and treating each room as its own design composition.

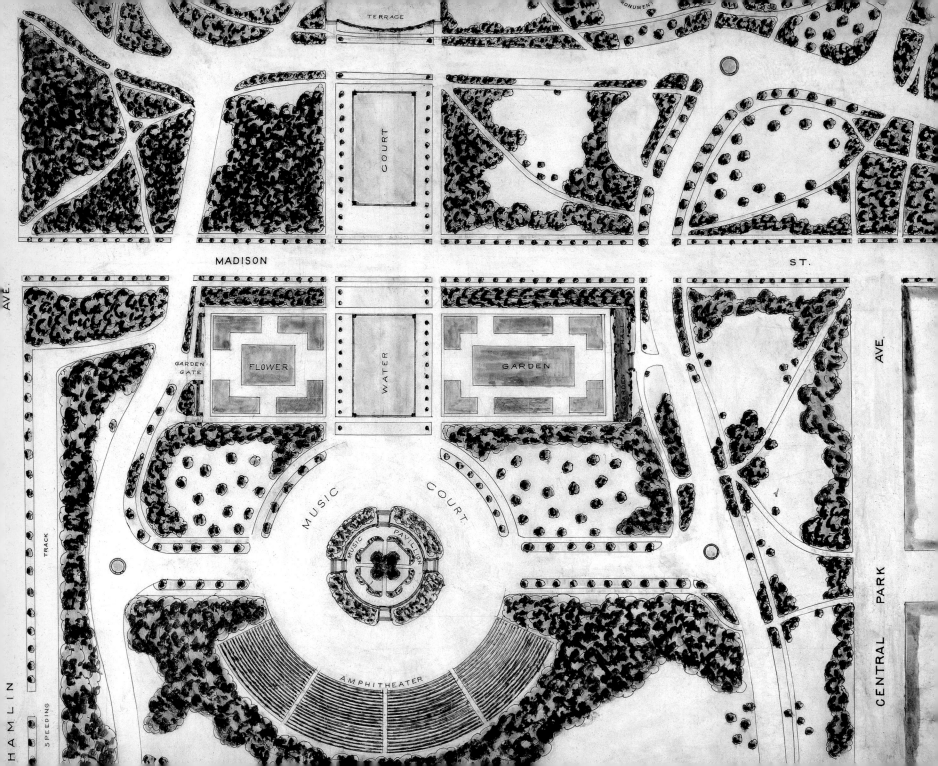

HARMONIOUS CONTRADICTIONS

Jensen's introduction of formal gardens in each of the three large parks seemed to be at odds with his belief that "every detail of the park composition should be in absolute harmony."[28] Blending straight lines, geometric forms, and rigid symmetry with Prairie-style landscape elements posed something of a contradiction. But in redesigning Humboldt, Garfield, and Douglas parks, Jensen felt that the public wanted fanciful gardens. Even though he later called these formal gardens "the folly of my youth," they were unlike any other gardens of the day.[29]

In Garfield Park, Jensen sited the new garden next to the old exotic bandstand. Although conventional in its cross-axial layout and use of some exotic flowers, the garden deviated from tradition by including Prairie style pergolas (trellis-like structures) and edging some beds with native plant material. The garden had rectangular water courts that produced a misty spray. Jensen said that "on sunny days a rainbow played continuously across the top of it. There would always be a crowd of people watching this."[30]

In 1907, State Architect William Carbys Zimmerman designed a boat house on the north end of the garden near the lagoon. The building had a low-hipped roof and octagonal open-pavilions on each end as well as arched openings from which boats were launched. Although Zimmerman is generally known for his eclectic Revival-style mansions, under Jens Jensen's influence he created this structure in the Prairie style. Unfortunately, fire destroyed the building in 1981, and without it the visual connection between the garden and lagoon has been lost.

Opposite page: *Preliminary Sketches for Proposed Improvements in Garfield Park*, Jens Jensen, ca. 1907. This page, left: Formal garden and water courts looking north to the bandstand, 1909. This page, right: Formal garden looking west, ca. 1935.

ARTS AND CULTIVATION

Jensen had deep reverence for the arts, but he did not feel that all works of sculpture were appropriate for his parks. Concerned that the "artistic insufficiency of the average frock-coated statues and prancing bronze soldiers" would mar the landscape, he asked members of the Municipal Art League of Chicago to evaluate specific sculpture proposals.[31] In 1906, the arts organization approved the installation of a monument to the Scottish poet Robert Burns south of the lagoon.

Two years later, the West Park Commission worked with the Municipal Art League and the Art Institute of Chicago to hold an outdoor art exhibit in Humboldt Park. This was so successful that a similar event was held in Garfield Park in 1909. Exploring appropriate settings for artworks, the two outdoor exhibits featured small plaster versions of sculptures that had been in the *World's Columbian Exposition* of 1893. Edward Kemeys' bison sculptures were placed in the entryway of the Garfield Park formal garden. Years later, these were recast in bronze, and moved to Humboldt Park. At that time, two sculptures of bulls with Indian maidens by Daniel Chester French and Edward C. Potter were installed in their place,

Left: *Bull with Indian Maiden* sculpture, 1936. Garfield Park's pair of bronze sculptures are much smaller than the original plaster versions from the *World's Columbian Exposition*. This one represents *Ceres*, the Roman goddess of grain. Right: *Robert Burns* monument in front of old Garfield Park Refectory, 1906.

flanking the garden. In the mid-1980s, vandals stole one of the bull sculptures and damaged the other. In 2003, conservator Andrzej Dajnowski recreated the missing sculpture and repaired the damaged one, reinstalling them in the City Garden behind the conservatory.

One of Jensen's favorite sculptors was Charles Mulligan, a protégé of the acclaimed Chicago artist, Lorado Taft. Mulligan sculpted *Lincoln the Railsplitter.* Honoring the revered president's modest beginnings, the monument was installed in Garfield Park in 1911.

CELEBRATING NATURE

Jensen was not only interested in having people view his landscapes; he wanted visitors to be uplifted and transformed by them. He vigorously promoted programs and events that celebrated art and nature. During the 1910s, the American pageantry movement was at its peak. The use of elaborate costumed dramas or parades was an effective way of attracting public attention to various causes at the time. In June of 1915, the West Park Commission sponsored a festival in Garfield Park. This *Pageant of the Year* was likely inspired by Jensen

Children in costumes in the *Pageant of the Year*, 1915. This procession of children dressed as garden flowers, butterflies, bees, humming birds, and grasshoppers, danced and skipped merrily through the park representing the light-heartedness of spring.

Women portraying Columbia and the Thirteen Original States at *Pageant of the Year*, 1915. The West Park Commissioners asserted that this event, with more than a thousand participants and approximately 25,000 spectators, represented America as the "Melting Pot of the world."

who had recently formed an organization that used pageantry as a vehicle to save natural areas. The Friends of Our Native Landscape met regularly at sites threatened by development and held similar outdoor festivals to attract attention to the need for conservation.

The theme of Garfield Park's pageant was nature and the four seasons. Each season was represented symbolically. Winter, for example, featured "…snowflakes and snow elves. Winter made way for *Father Time and the New Year*, attended by little girls representing the twelve months. A profusion of snowbirds, snowmen, snowballs, holly and mistletoe romped."[32] The procession of 1,400 costumed children and adults wove its way through the park.

JENSEN OUSTED AGAIN

In 1920, political winds shifted again when Governor Frank O. Lowden removed all seven members of the West Park Board of Commissioners from office. He accused the board of improper campaigning for local politicians and extravagant spending. Jensen's annual salary and reimbursements of more than $5,000 were perceived as too high.[33] Aware that he would soon be ousted, Jensen severed his ties with the West Park Commission for the final

Rendering from Jens Jensen's plan for *A Greater West Park System*, 1920.

time. Unfortunately for Chicago, this happened in the midst of his most creative period. He had recently designed his masterpiece, Columbus Park, and was completing an ambitious plan to add thousands of acres of additional green space to the city's West Side. Leaving his public position, Jensen turned to a thriving private practice. By this time, his client list included many successful businessmen such as Harold Florsheim, Ogden Armour, Henry Ford and his son, Edsel.

THE ROARING TWENTIES

During the 1920s, Chicago grew into a bustling city of more than three million residents. With the rise of industry, congested neighborhoods, and the increasing presence of the automobile, parks became even more important in urban life. In these prosperous and optimistic times, West Siders enjoyed a variety of activities in Garfield Park throughout the year. Social dancing, concerts, card parties, and Bunco (a popular dice game) were favorite pastimes.

Wading pool and lawn tennis south of conservatory, 1917.

In wintertime, Garfield Park had ice boat races, "barrel stave ski contests," tobogganing on a large wooden chute that was erected annually, and ice skating.[34] Popular ice skating events on the frozen lagoon included the *Chicago Tribune Silver Skates Derby*, *Daily News Ice Skating Carnival*, and Mayor Thompson's *Inter-City Skating Tournament*. Some of these attracted as many as 30,000 spectators.[35]

Garfield Park's summers were also very lively, with boating, fishing and golf, which could be played on the links for ten cents a game. A natatorium built at the northwest side of the park had swimming and wading pools. Roque, a game similar to croquet, was another popular diversion in the park.

During the late 1920s, the commissioners began planning several improvements, especially focusing on ornate buildings. In 1928, a ten-million dollar bond issue funded improvements throughout the West Park System. Michaelsen & Rognstad, local architects of Norwegian descent, designed three fanciful buildings in Garfield Park—a warehouse and shop structure, an expanded Roque facility (later demolished) and a striking new administrative headquarters.

Top left: Children wearing costumes and ices skates at the *Chicago Daily News Mardi Gras and Skating Carnival*, 1929. Top right: Costumed woman in *Mardi Gras and Skating Carnival*, 1929. Bottom: Woman teeing off at Garfield Park golf course, 1929.

"I only went out once; they still had skating
in my grammar school years. I don't know
about high school. I went with a girlfriend,
an immigrant from out of state or something;
anyway she wasn't Jewish so she knew how
to skate. So I could barely stand up on the
skates…but at least I had that experience,
that all American sort of old-timey skating
experience."

—Beverly Chubat, Editor, Chicago Jewish History

"In the winter, if it was really cold the lake would
freeze, because you had to make sure the ice
was thick enough and there were hundreds of
people at city-wide skating meets. We had short
blades but the racers had long blades. I talked
my dad into getting me skates like racers had."

—George J. Cotsirilos

Garfield Park Silver Skates speed skating event, 1937.

GOLD DOME BUILDING

The West Park Commissioners decided that their own headquarters would be the most elaborate and expensive. They selected Garfield Park because of its central location in the system, and a special art committee recommended the dramatic lagoon site. Michaelsen & Rognstad designed the administration building in an eclectic Spanish Revival style that was popular throughout America at that time. The east façade strongly resembles the California Building of San Diego's 1915 Panama-California Exposition. Garfield Park's iconic building, with its enormous gold leaf dome, reaches a height of ninety feet.

The lavish building has rich details made of cut stone, terra cotta, ornamental plaster-work, and terrazzo. Bronze sculptures of Midwestern explorer Robert Cavalier de La Salle, Christopher Columbus, and an unidentified figure decorate the entryway. Inside, bas relief panels enliven the rotunda walls. The panels celebrate the achievements of the twentieth century such as modern roadways, art and architecture, parks and playgrounds. In one, allegorical figures in togas representing "art" and "architecture" are holding up a representation of this elaborate Garfield Park building. The bas relief panels were sculpted by Richard W. Bock (1865–1949) who was especially famous for collaborating with architect Frank Lloyd Wright on many projects including Wright's home and studio in Oak Park.

In addition to offices for commissioners and staff, the Gold Dome building originally had a squad room for park police, holding cells for offenders, and a garage. It also provided a warming area for ice skaters, boat storage, and a concession booth. After the formation of the Chicago Park District in 1934, administrative offices were no longer needed in Garfield Park, and the monumental building became a cultural and recreational facility.

DEPRESSION-ERA PARK CONSOLIDATION

Before the Chicago Park District was first created, the West Park System was one of twenty-two separate park districts operating simultaneously in the city. Along with the problems caused by such an unwieldy number of agencies, there were compelling financial reasons for consolidation. The Depression had rendered most, if not all of these independent park commissions financially insolvent. To gain access to federal funding through President Franklin Delano Roosevelt's New Deal, voters approved the Park Consolidation Act of 1934 that unified all of the individual districts into a single agency.

Between 1935 and 1941, the Chicago Park District received more than $82 million in federal funding through Project Works Administration (PWA) and the Works Progress

Opposite page: Looking north across the lagoon towards Gold Dome building, ca. 1935. This page: Front facade of Gold Dome building, ca. 1940.

Administration (WPA). State and City funds increased this total to more than $100 million.[36] Using these funds, the park district made numerous improvements throughout the system.

WPA-FUNDED WORK IN GARFIELD PARK

Many WPA projects focused on traffic improvements, upgrading recreational facilities, and repairing and replanting the parks. At the time, the adjacent West Jackson Boulevard was often congested, and cars had to take a detour around the park. The Chicago Motor Club suggested cutting West Jackson Boulevard through the golf course to alleviate the problem. The Park District agreed, building a new West Jackson Boulevard extension and converting the golf links into two smaller athletic fields. The new more convenient roadway also brought noise and traffic into the landscape.

The West Jackson Boulevard extension destroyed some of the Jensen-designed landscape, but his influence was not completely lost. In the 1930s, the Chicago Park District had a talented staff of designers who had a deep understanding of Jensen's contributions. The landscape design staff believed in using "native material and creating natural effects" especially in the large parks.[37] They planted tens of thousands of trees and shrubs in Garfield Park and restored the edges of the lagoon. There was a conscious effort to educate the

Left: West Jackson Boulevard looking east from South Hamlin Avenue before extension, May 5, 1936. Right: West Jackson Boulevard extension through Garfield Park during construction, November 11, 1936.

"My mother and I were on the
bridge watching the boats rowing
in the lagoon. She leaned over and
her watch fell in the water. We
had to get the man from the Park
District to get it out."

—Zelda Bachrach

"The lagoon was a great attraction
and in the summer there were
rowboats. If you had a girlfriend
you'd take her rowing."

—George J. Cotsirilos

"My mother brought us to this
park as children. They had boats
here and I learned how to row.
I don't even know how my mom
got started rowing boats. It was
in the mid-1930s."

—Reverend Eudora Ramey

Rowboats on lagoon, 1919.

foremen about the aesthetic values and scientific aspects of native plants. The designers found that the field workers were more respectful and cooperative when they had a clear understanding of the naturalistic philosophies behind the plantings.

JOIE DE VIVRE IN THE PARK

While life was difficult for many Chicagoans during the throes of the Depression, Garfield Park offered many uplifting diversions. Federal relief funding helped provide an array of sports and cultural programs. Swimming meets, lessons, and water polo took place in the natatorium, while the fields were frequently used for baseball, softball, rugby, football, and soccer. The Chicago Fly Casting Club continued holding tournaments that had long included women as members. The *Silver Skates* competition expanded its race divisions for girls in 1936.[38]

Large festivals in Garfield Park such as the *Water Carnival and Venetian Night* helped take people's minds off of their troubles. Park patrons made illuminated water floats. While these drifted in the lagoon, people in giant paper maché "grotesque heads" escorted Miss Garfield Park and her maids of court.

Top: Garfield Park women's bicycle event, ca. 1937. Bottom left: Dancers on terrace of Gold Dome building, ca. 1937. Bottom right: Garfield Park day camp, ca. 1940. Chief Whirling Thunder, a Winnebago Indian, taught crafts, archery, and Indian lore at various parks.

Left: Acrobats performing on the terrace of the Gold Dome building, ca. 1937. Right: "Taj Mahal" water float, 1935. Such water floats were produced as WPA art projects and placed in the park lagoons.

Arts and crafts and other activities took place in the Gold Dome, which had now become the park's field house. The building also headquartered the first branch galleries of the Art Institute of Chicago. Exhibits focused on American and European art of the nineteenth and twentieth centuries. Some of the shows included original paintings by Van Gogh, Renoir, and other masters. Sculpture and photography, oil paintings, and sketches from the Museum of Modern Art in New York were featured, as well as works by WPA artists from Chicago.[39] The Garfield Park Art Galleries remained for three years.

WWII AND ITS IMPACT ON THE PARK

In December of 1941, after America entered World War II, the Chicago Park District shifted its focus to the war effort. Each of the city's ninety-six field houses provided "…a hub of civilian defense activities in its respective community."[40] American Red Cross training was given to the public at the Gold Dome. Garfield Park also became an important place for thousands of servicemen, particularly because the Illinois Reserve militia provided training for its members there. As part of the program, they staged mock air raids in the park.

After World War II, veterans and other citizens continued to hold memorials in Garfield Park. The American Legion sponsored the *Here's Your Infantry Show* that demonstrated World War II tactics and weaponry in 1945.[41] Members also helped organize an annual parade that culminated in a ceremony at the *American Doughboy* Monument near North Hamlin Boulevard and West Madison Street in Garfield Park. This monument had been donated after World War I to honor soldiers of the 132nd infantry. It remained a symbol for veterans of both world wars, until it was severely vandalized, removed, and put in storage by the early 1970s. In 2003, the sculpture was conserved and installed near Gate O in Soldier Field.

CONTINUITY AND CHANGE

After World War II, favorite pastimes in Garfield Park continued to be parades, athletic events, and arts and cultural activities as the surrounding community was changing. The early populations of Northern European and Irish immigrants had largely shifted to Italians and Jews. By the 1950s, some of the neighborhoods near Garfield Park were becoming racially integrated as well.

For years, the vicinity's African Americans rarely frequented events and classes in Garfield Park. Rather, they participated in Union Park's programs which were staffed by black professionals. Larger numbers of black residents began to use Garfield Park in the 1950s, when the finals for many city-wide tournaments were held there. These competitions provided a positive vehicle for bringing children of different races and backgrounds together. Some of the park's most popular championships were marbles and horse-shoe games. Park District tennis clinics also began attracting African American participants in the late 1950s.

Left: Chicago Park District tennis clinic in Garfield Park, 1954. Right: Winners of city-wide marbles tournament in Garfield Park, 1958.

Left: City-wide tennis championship in Garfield Park, 1955. Betty Harris presents trophy to winner, Helen Mayes. Right: Boy on parallel bars in Garfield Park gymnastics program, ca. 1980.

The post-war baby boom resulted in a larger population of young children in the area but the West Side lacked some of the basic services that it needed the most. The Chicago Park District tried to use Garfield Park to help fill the void. The commissioners approved the construction of Leif Ericson School in 1963 on the southeast edge of the park to help alleviate overcrowding of the area's schools. At the same time, they allowed the Board of Health to open a clinic in the Gold Dome building.

The Gold Dome provided more than health services. It also continued as a mecca for arts and cultural programming. In the late 1960s, Garfield Park had an African American park supervisor, John Houston, who had grown up in Union Park and graduated from the Goodman School of Drama. Houston used theatrical programs to engender black pride. His Garfield Park Players performed the work of Langston Hughes along with other important African American playwrights in the Gold Dome, and at Lincoln Park's Theater on the Lake.

DECADES OF VIGOR AND DECLINE

In the 1970s and 1980s, park systems throughout the nation increasingly focused on active recreation. In Garfield Park, football, softball, boxing, fishing derbies, day camp, and the acclaimed drama club were some of the most popular activities. The Park District built new tennis courts and held clinics and tournaments. In 1973, a Garfield Park event featured black tennis superstar Althea Gibson who excited neighborhood children about her sport.[42] Facilities for other sports were also being expanded. In 1984, the small natatorium west of the conservatory was replaced by a large addition to the Gold Dome building with a full-size indoor gym and an outdoor swimming pool.

During this era, the national zeal for park programming often came at the expense of facilities and landscapes. In urban parks, such neglect was compounded by the increasing socioeconomic problems of inner cities. Graffiti was becoming more pervasive in Garfield Park and metal and bronze elements were regularly vandalized. With increasing crime rates, security became a higher priority, bringing more fencing, harsh lighting, and the removal of shrubbery. Dutch Elm Disease, higher labor costs, and a loss of craftsmanship took a toll on Garfield Park's beautifully designed historic landscapes. The Chicago Park District was ill-equipped to deal with these complex issues, especially because a political patronage system allowed many incompetent and indolent employees to keep their jobs.

Activists pointed out that the parks within minority communities such as the West Side were especially neglected. In the early 1980s, citizens and civic groups filed a formal complaint against the Chicago Park District with the United States District Court. This document asserted that the Park District's policies and practices discriminated against residents of African American and Latino communities.[43] The dispute was settled through a consent decree, resulting in an intensive study and a series of remedies. Among these were decentralizing the management of the parks, dividing resources and staff more equitably, improving landscapes and facilities, and adopting a system of citizen-based advisory councils. The newly formed Garfield Park Advisory Council soon played an active role in improving and managing the park.

Left: Boxing match, ca. 1980. Right: View of garden wall showing graffiti and deterioration, ca. 1980.

"I played ping-pong at the
Gold Dome…I used to take
a girlfriend there and we had
vicious ping-pong games.

—Dr. Irving Cutler

"In 1949, maybe 1950, I was
dating and my boyfriend had
a car. So we would come and
park right in front of the Gold
Dome, and look at the water,
and we'd talk—no hanky
panky in the car."

—Nettie Bailey

Gold Dome building and lagoon, 2005.

NURTURING NATURE

The 1990s brought new vitality to Garfield Park—largely inspired by the people who live in the surrounding community. The park was officially listed on the National Register of Historic Places in 1993, and the community became increasingly vocal about the need to preserve this important historic site. After much urging from the Garfield Park Advisory Council, the Park District began restoring and regilding the Gold Dome. Millions of dollars of park improvements followed. In 1997, the Park District conducted an extensive lagoon rehabilitation project which took an innovative ecological approach. The Garfield Park Conservatory Alliance is an important partner with the Park District in efforts to restore the conservatory, enhance the greater park, and improve its programming.

New cultural activities have been flourishing through partnerships with the Alvin Ailey Dance Troupe, Najwa Dance Company, and the Chicago West Music Center. The Park District offers movies and concerts in the park, day camp, basketball, boxing, and other sports. For several years beginning in 2000, the Peace Museum operated out of the Gold Dome building, until it outgrew its space there. This vacancy made way for a much-needed teen program featuring video production and film making.

In 2003, the Chicago Park District Advisory Council, other community groups, and consultants produced a Garfield Park Framework Plan that identifies the park's assets and presents a vision for its future development and management. The Garfield Park Conservatory Alliance and the Park District have also sparked several other planning initiatives that embrace the conservatory as a catalyst for improvements not only to Garfield Park but to the entire West Side. ✦

Left: Alvin Ailey Dance Camp performance, 2001.
Right: Movie in the park, 2006.

"In May, 1941, my parents, Ben and Laila Alajoki, set up there first apartment as newlyweds just off the corner of Lake Street and Central Park, across the street from the Garfield Park Conservatory. My mother, fresh from a farm in northern Minnesota, was enchanted by the exotic plants in the greenhouses, and visited them often during her first year of marriage."
—Jean Sanno

"The conservatory is a wonderful resource and shouldn't be allowed to go to rot and ruin."

—Mary Nelson, Past President, Bethel New Life

"I felt we had a responsibility to leave these beautiful places of recreation and respite better than we found them. Being a West Sider, I felt that restoring the Garfield Park Conservatory was especially important."

—Michael W. Scott, Former President,
Chicago Park District Board of Commissioners

Aerial view of Garfield Park Conservatory
during reglazing project, 2003.

"Well, when I was a child we used to go there, maybe '42 to '53 that I remember really well. We would sell newspapers on the street corner during the day and in the evening but in the summer we used the park a lot. We had the big lagoons and we used to go fishing. Right in the lagoons we'd catch perch and other fish."

—Vincent Alloco

"For fifty some years I've been fishing in the lagoons. There was a time where you could stay out there all night long. You took your family on the hot days and you'd picnic all night long. I mostly get catfish, also blue gill. Always drive because I have my equipment. Go home, clean them up, freeze them. Come home with twenty-five or thirty fish, after that I don't feel like eating them. A lot of them I give to my friends, then I don't have to clean them."

—Mello Sam

Fishing in Garfield Park lagoon, 2007. The Illinois Department of Natural Resources stocks the park lagoons with channel catfish, large mouth bass, and bluegill.

"When I am at the conservatory I feel safe, and I know that no one or anything can harm me…I am safe and this wonderful scenery encloses me. It sort of feels like I am [in] paradise. It's a calm and wonderful feeling."

—Ashley M., Green Teen, age 14

"Being inspired by nature is like being touched in your dream. It's love for something that goes all the way down to the core of your heart."

—Sirah D., Green Teen, age 14

Green Teens at the Garfield Park Conservatory, 2007.

"I played tackle football for the Garfield Park Gators. I can recall one game I played in Garfield Park on the football field. It was my very first game as a Gator. It was cold, and lots of parents were there. The field was very muddy. I played my heart out."

—Lomont R., Willa Cather Elementary School

"We would have a picnic every year. Large school picnic where the kids, the teachers, and everybody would get out and participate. We would have field games, you know, track and field, and throwing the softball, throwing the football, and that kinda stuff, right there all day long. It was something that the kids really enjoyed."

—Demetrius Armstrong,
    Former Teacher, Lucy Flower High School

Al Raby High School football team practicing in Garfield Park, 2007.

"My favorite thing to do is play basketball on the court when the summer comes. I really love to play one-on-one with my cousin. One day I dunked on my cousin and he laughed about it because it was my first time. Dunking on an eight-foot rim is my special memory…In the summer I come to the park as often as I can."

—Eddie J., Green Teen, age 17

"I was on a basketball team for Garfield Park and we tried to win every game we played. I played softball there too. We went to the final round, but we got beat."

—Reginald J., Willa Cather Elementary School

"All of the neighborhood kids would go to the Golden Dome and watch the different neighborhood kids play on the basketball team. This was really fun because everyone used to come and just hang out and have fun watching the game."

—Yolandis M., Green Teen, age 14

Garfield Park basketball court, 2007.

"I went swimming at the Golden Dome. I also visited the summer camp program there. There is a gym and an art room. There are many other activities you can do such as volleyball, cooking classes, and many other things…You can play in the park or have a picnic."

—Tameka M., Willa Cather Elementary School

"At Garfield Park, I had a lot of fun…Every morning I went there to swim until the summer was over."

—Reginald J., Willa Cather Elementary School

"I think that the pond is a beautiful sight… I loved seeing the pond and all of the people taking advantage of the exciting activities for young people."

—Breona H., Willa Cather Elementary School

Garfield Park swimming pool and lagoon, 2004.

"As a high school student I spent many afternoons at the conservatory. I loved living near such beauty. It was always so full of life and fun…I was always so proud that I lived near such a beautiful home of all those plants and flowers."

—Mary Scott-Boria

"Books, we need. But if you want a breath of fresh air, you will not get it out of a book. It will be [from] falling in love with nature."

—Reverend Ramey

"This was a beautiful park and it is still is. Today it's been renewed—this park has gone through a death, dying, and resurrection."

—Vincent Alloco

City Garden, 2006.

GARFIELD PARK IS ONE OF THE FIRST AMERICAN PARKS to have a public conservatory in its original plan. Conceived in 1870, a small but fanciful glass house was built there in the following decade. After that structure fell into disrepair, Jens Jensen replaced it with an amazingly innovative facility. Unlike typical greenhouses with showy displays of potted plants, his conservatory had tropical plantings placed directly in the ground, stratified stonework, lagoons, and cascading water. Considered revolutionary when it opened in 1908, visitors were "moved by exquisite scenes" that conveyed "an idea too deep for words."[1] In its second century, the Garfield Park Conservatory is becoming revolutionary once again as its role expands to more fully enrich people's lives beyond the glass walls.

Garfield Park Conservatory, ca. 1908.

View of Crystal Palace, 1851. Before designing the Crystal Palace, landscape gardener Joseph Paxton created the Great Conservatory at Chatsworth and then patented his method of glass construction. He designed the Crystal Palace in only ten days, for which he was granted knighthood.

CONSERVATORIES DEBUT IN EUROPE

In the early nineteenth century, new building technologies allowed for the construction of the first conservatories in Europe. Before this, there had been many attempts to create controlled environments to nurture and protect plants. By the seventeenth century, orangeries had become fashionable with European nobility. They used these rudimentary greenhouses to propagate fruit for their own estates. To house more extensive plant collections, better facilities were needed.

Public interest in horticulture was heightened by explorers who collected and classified exotic plants from continents such as Africa and Asia. This enthusiasm, along with advances in glass and iron construction, prompted the development of more substantial structures to display flowers and other plants. (During this period, some were made of wooden frames instead of iron.) Among premier examples were the Belfast Conservatory in Ireland, Jardin des Plantes in Paris, and the Palm House in England's Kew Gardens. These showy gardens under glass quickly captured the imagination of people throughout world.

One of the most famous was the Crystal Palace which housed the 1851 Great Exhibition in London. Landscape gardener Joseph Paxton designed the massive glass structure to house more than just plants. Exhibitry within the Crystal Palace showcased the achievements of the Industrial Revolution.

Ironically, fears about the Industrial Revolution contributed to the growing interest in conservatories. Worried that plants would disappear as factories encroached, urban dwellers wanted to visit nature in glass structures with lush display houses. Even those who did not share this concern were attracted to the caché of a conservatory in their own city. As Americans of the nineteenth century looked to Europe for fashionable ideas, it did not take long for the first conservatories to appear in the United States.

PIONEERING AMERICAN GREENHOUSES

In America, a carpenter named Frederick A. Lord began building greenhouses of wood and glass for estate owners in the 1850s. In 1867, the Massachusetts Agricultural College (now the University of Massachusetts) hired Lord to construct the pioneering Durfee Conservatory. This early public conservatory was meant to educate and inspire working-class people in Amherst and the surrounding area.

Lord continued building wood and glass conservatories throughout the nation with his son-in-law William Addison Burnham. In some cases, their conservatories were shipped across the country in sections designed to be assembled upon arrival. An early client, California piano manufacturer James Lick, purchased a Lord & Burnham conservatory in parts, but passed away in 1876, before he could build it. Several San Francisco businessmen acquired the unassembled pieces still packed in crates and erected the conservatory in what became Golden Gate Park.

In 1881, Lord & Burnham created the first metal-framed conservatory in America for railroad magnate Jay Gould. Now known as the Lyndhurst Conservatory, it still stands in Tarrytown, New York.

Durfee Conservatory, ca. 1880. Located in Amherst, Massachusetts, this was one of the first public conservatories in America.

Garfield Park Conservatory and surrounding gardens, 1897. Architects Fromann and Jebsen designed this exuberant Victorian structure.

EARLIEST CHICAGO CONSERVATORIES IN WEST PARKS

As early as 1870, William Le Baron Jenney had envisioned a fine conservatory for Chicago's Central Park. Convinced that the West Park Commissioners would soon receive gifts of plants and minerals from all over the world, he recommended a proper building "for their protection where they can be both classified and examined."[2] His original park plan called for an area focusing on natural history that was meant to include a winter garden with display and propagating houses.

This plan called for one of America's very first public conservatories, but funds fell short. Instead, in the mid-1870s, the commissioners built small utilitarian hothouses in Humboldt, Garfield, and Douglas parks. The structures were meant to provide "an adequate supply of flowers for proper embellishment" of the parks and boulevards.[3] They had no public show houses and within a decade, all three were severely dilapidated.

The commissioners began replacing the three greenhouses with larger public conservatories in the 1880s. Composed of wood and glass, each of these Victorian conservatories was rendered in its own exotic style, with public display houses and rooms for plant propagation. William Le Baron Jenney designed Douglas Park's conservatory, while the others were the work of Fromann and Jebsen, Chicago architects known for Romantic-style buildings.

Garfield Park's conservatory was the most substantial. The whimsical building had an impressive domed display house. Some visitors thought it looked like "…the United States Capitol in miniature."[4] An abundance of colored glass created a shimmering effect near the roof-line.

CONSERVATORIES CATCH ON IN CHICAGO

As enthusiasm for conservatories continued to grow, efforts were underway to build some in other parts of Chicago. On the North Side, the Lincoln Park Commissioners erected a conservatory designed by Joseph Lyman Silsbee, with trusses in the shape of ogee arches, a form with associations to the Near East. This historic structure remains popular today.

In 1893, a massive conservatory, the Horticulture Building, materialized in Jackson Park for the *World's Columbian Exposition*. Jenney designed this impressive temporary structure in the Italian Renaissance style. It housed enormous floral displays, orange and lemon groves, and even a replica of South Dakota's Mammoth Crystal Cave in its central rotunda. The building was razed after the World's Fair, but many of its plants were saved, leading to the creation of a conservatory in Washington Park. This Lord & Burnham structure opened in 1897. Although it was meant to be permanent, the Chicago Park District demolished the Washington Park Conservatory in the 1930s.

DECREPIT GLASS HOUSES

By the turn of the century, there were five conservatories in Chicago but problems abounded. The glass houses in Humboldt, Garfield, and Douglas parks were less than twenty years old, and they were already falling apart. The old Garfield Park Conservatory's wooden structure—held together "by braces and trusses of all sorts"—was so rotted that in places "an investigator was able to thrust his finger into it."[5] Conditions at the other two were equally disastrous. This wasn't completely surprising considering that the old conservatories were difficult buildings to maintain, especially in Chicago's climate.

In 1904, the West Park Commissioners considered replacing the three decrepit glass houses with a superior central conservatory. They could not take action, however, because their scandalous mismanagement of the park system had recently been exposed. The following year, a new board appointed Jens Jensen as general superintendent. He viewed the old greenhouses as boring and redundant in their plant collections, and was excited about the idea of replacing them with a single premier facility in Garfield Park. A $160,000 budget made his ambitions possible. He planned a structure with a floor area covering more than 68,000 square feet and an additional 30,000 square feet of propagating houses. These dimensions would make it the largest facility of its kind in the world.

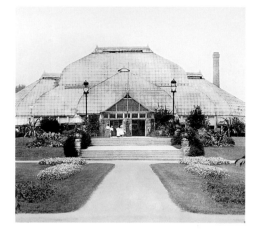

Lincoln Park Conservatory, ca. 1895. Joseph Lyman Silsbee designed the Lincoln Park Conservatory, which still exists today.

A NEW DIRECTION

Jensen contemplated an entirely new direction for his conservatory. He did not want it "…to look like a palace, a chateau, or a Renaissance villa," typical of the showy glass houses of the period.[6] Instead, his conservatory's form was inspired by "the great haystacks which are so eloquent of the richness of prairie soil."[7] To collaborate on the structure's design, Jensen hired Hitchings & Company, a New York engineering firm that specialized in greenhouses. He also commissioned Prairie School architects Schmidt, Garden, & Martin to design an elegant vestibule and interior decorative details. (These were later demolished.)

Even more noteworthy than its architectural design was the artistic treatment of the interior. The new Garfield Park Conservatory was conceived by Jensen as a work of landscape art under glass. Other conservatories of the period were like museums with exotic species in pots clumped together in the middle of their show houses. In contrast, Jensen kept the center of each room open, creating scenic views, and framing them with plants and stonework. He planted directly into the ground, a relatively new practice for conservatories. Most importantly, he treated the rooms as though they were outdoor landscapes, designing each as its own composition.

The structure had seven original rooms. There was a massive Palm House that connected with a series of display rooms: the Stove, New Holland, Economic, Conifer, and Show houses. Arranged in the form of a quadrangle, these rooms surrounded the structure's premier space—the Aquatic House—later called the Fern Room.

Palm House reflecting pool, 1907. Schmidt, Garden, & Martin's original water feature had Art Glass lanterns.

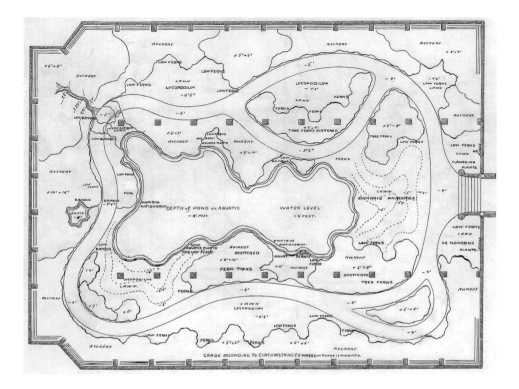

Top: *Proposed Plan for Aquatic and Rockery Display in Conservatory*, Jens Jensen, 1907. Bottom: *Proposed Range of Conservatories to be Erected in Garfield Park, East Elevation*, Hitchings & Co., ca. 1907.

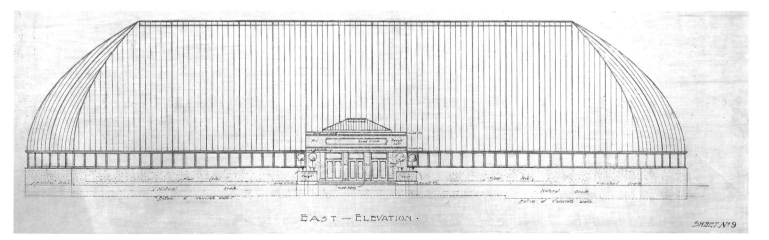

EAST — ELEVATION·

"I used the conservatory for a movie one time. It was called *The Monitors*. We needed a tropical setting and it was low-budget."

—Bernard Sahlins,
    Founder, The Second City

"I think it inspires people to be more centered, more at peace with themselves. The atmosphere in the place is quiet, peaceful…the flowing water, the fish in the little ponds."

—Vincent Alloco

Fern Room looking northeast, 1909.

IDEALIZED PRAIRIE LANDSCAPES

Within the conservatory, Jensen conveyed his Prairie style through elements such as water features, stratified stonework, and an emphasis on horizontality. The entrance of the Palm House provided an exquisite view across a curved water court into the sunken Fern Room. In the center of that room, Jensen designed a lagoon edged by stratified stonework. To frame the scene, he placed low-growing plants Lycopodium and Selaginella in the foreground, with larger ferns and cycads layered above. Liberty Hyde Bailey, the pre-eminent American horticulturalist described the room:

> "…the tree-ferns overhead and the selaginellas as a ground cover, are used in
> large numbers to make bands of foliage to arch paths and hide the glass roof,
> and to frame in vistas to glimpses of water, carpets of green below."[8]

The water not only offered magnificent views, but also cleverly provided necessary moisture for the plants. Mosses, lichens, ferns, and other vegetation grew freely on the crevices of the stone. In addition to supporting plant life, the beautiful limestone ledges helped hide the ugly pipes and mechanical systems necessary in a greenhouse.

At the far end of the room, Jensen created an idealized "prairie waterfall" made of layers of stratified stone.[9] He designed the waterfall to serve as the symbolic source of the lagoon. A stepping stone path crossed a little brook to bring visitors right up to the waterfall, a place that appealed to several senses at once.

Left: Fern Room looking west, ca. 1910. This view shows the "carpet of green" in the foreground. Right: Liberty Hyde Bailey at the Garfield Park Conservatory, ca. 1945.

Top: Garfield Park Conservatory gardeners, 1913.
Bottom: Fern Room looking east, 1908. Jensen
criticized this photograph. On the back, he wrote,
this is a "head on view which destroys all poetry."

The renowned landscape architect wanted his prairie waterfall to sound just right. During its construction, Jensen was displeased because he thought it sounded like "an abrupt mountain cascade."[10] After directing the mason to dismantle and rebuild the waterfall several times, the workman became terribly frustrated. Jensen suggested that he ask someone to play Mendelssohn's *Spring Song* on the piano. The man went home that night and told his wife "Jensen's gone cracked."[11] His opinion changed once he heard the music. The next day, the mason went back to work and constructed the stonework perfectly so that the "water tinkled gently from ledge to ledge, as it should in a prairie country."[12]

Although the use of tropical plants might seem incongruous to Jensen's Prairie style, the Garfield Park Conservatory's collections actually tied into his design ethos. In 1915, Wilhelm Miller, a professor of landscape architecture, explained that its rooms represented prehistoric Illinois. "The idea is poetical—to suggest the tropical beauty of prairie-land before the coming of man."[13]

Fern Room waterfall, ca. 1908. The man-made stonework looked so real that visitors often thought the conservatory had been built around a natural spring.

ORIGINAL PLANT COLLECTIONS

Jensen wanted the new conservatory to house a much more interesting collection of plants than the earlier ones had. The modern facility provided different rooms with special temperatures and humidity necessary for "plants from all parts of the warmer zones of the earth."[14]

The Palm House, filled with vegetation from the tropics, had many favorites of the period such as date, fish tail, and sago palms as well as bamboo and cocoa trees. The Fern Room featured tree ferns that came from a large plant family thought to be in danger of extinction. These, along with several 250-year old cycads, were among the most valuable in the collection. Some of the rarest plants, including the cycads, were acquired from a New Jersey plant collector. The West Park Commissioners purchased these plants "at a considerable discount" after they had been exhibited at the 1908 Flower Show in Chicago's Coliseum.[15]

The Stove House, commonly known as the Warm House, had tender plants such as Anthurium, Nepenthes, and Diffenbachia. A large group of subtropical evergreens including Auracarius grew in the Conifer House. The Economic House displayed plants that were used for products and food such as lemon, pepper, and rubber trees. The New Holland House had the bottle brush and other plants from the Australian islands, an area popularized by Dutch explorers. Flowering plants and special flower shows flourished in the Show House.

FLOWER SHOWS

In early April of 1908, the new Garfield Park Conservatory opened to the public in time for Easter. All of the rooms were not ready, but visitors were allowed in the Show House. It featured a special exhibit of spring flowers such as tulips, azaleas, hyacinths, and rhododendrons.

The following year, a tradition of three annual flower shows began. The *Mid-Winter Show* celebrated the Christmas holidays with poinsettias, Christmas pepper, and the rare Glore de Lorraine begonia. The autumn *Chrysanthemum Show* featured hundreds of specimens of mums and the *Spring Show* provided a profusion of blossoming Easter lilies, golden daffodils, jonquils, and Persian violets. Because the seasonal flower shows were extremely popular, the West Park Commission opened the conservatory from eight o'clock in the morning to ten o'clock at night. The shows generally ran for two weeks but were often extended for longer periods.

GREAT DOME OF WOOD AND PUTTY

In September of 1909, only a year and a half after Jensen's conservatory had opened, its tremendous glass roof needed to be completely reconstructed. Although the building's massive metal trusses remained sound, its glazing system was failing. The roof's lapped glass panes had been puttied into a wooden framework that had been built with inferior wood.

This page: Original construction of Conifer House, ca.1908. This later became the Aroid House. Opposite page: A flower show in Garfield Park Conservatory's Show House, ca. 1908.

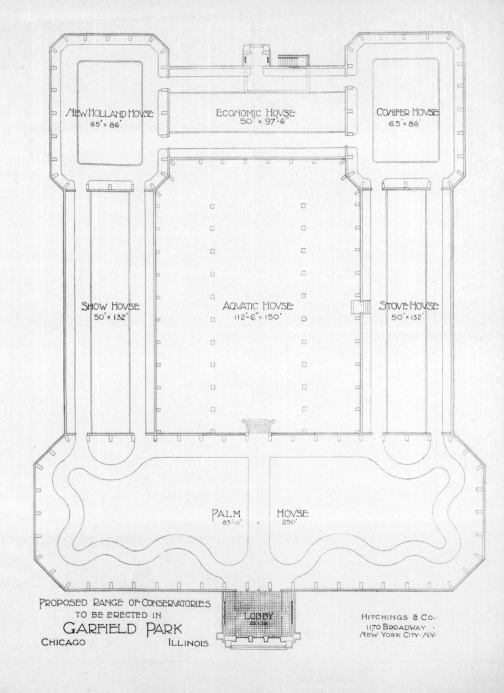

Left: Conifer House, 1910. Right: Floor Plan, Hitchings & Co., 1906. This early plan was followed in every respect except for the placement of the Stove and Show houses. In the original construction, the rooms were flipped, with the Stove House on the left side and Show House on the right. The Aquatic House became known as the Fern Room.

NEW HOLLAND HOUSE
65' x 86'

ECONOMIC HOUSE
50' x 97'-6"

CONIFER HOUSE
65' x 86'

SHOW HOUSE
50' x 132'

AQUATIC HOUSE
112'-6" x 150'

STOVE HOUSE
50' x 132'

PALM
85'-0"   x

HOUSE
250'

PROPOSED RANGE OF CONSERVATORIES
TO BE ERECTED IN
GARFIELD PARK
CHICAGO   ILLINOIS

LOBBY
25' x 58'

HITCHINGS & CO.
1170 BROADWAY
NEW YORK CITY · N.Y.

The *Chicago Tribune* reported that the great glass dome, "now rickety and riddled with holes is in danger of collapse."[16]

Jensen faulted the West Park Commissioners because they didn't hire a contractor with special conservatory expertise. The commissioners blamed him because he supervised the contractors and approved all of their construction materials. The State Board of Architects suggested that the building failed because its plans had not been prepared by a licensed architect. (Schmidt, Garden & Martin had only designed the front vestibule.)

In the fall of 1909, the head gardener warned that "the vast collection of tropical plants in the conservatory was in imminent peril, and would be destroyed if a new dome were not put up before winter."[17] The commissioners moved swiftly, hiring architect Henry Sierks to design a new glazing system for the conservatory. Sierks' new glass roofs utilized heavier cypress glazing bars, copper caps to clamp the glass in place, and copper gutters that would provide better drainage. This system no longer relied on lapping the glass panes. The seventy-five thousand dollar repair took a year to complete and was successful despite some injury to the tree ferns and Jensen's reputation. In response to growing tensions with the board, Jensen voluntarily shifted his role from superintendent to consulting landscape architect.

"LITTLE WHIMSIES"

The restored conservatory quickly became so popular that the commissioners widened the adjacent road and embellished the front entrance with a new water court and flowers. In 1913, a new pair of marble sculptures by artist Lorado Taft greeted visitors once they entered the Palm House. Named *Pastoral* and *Idyl*, these sculptures replaced earlier temporary plaster versions.

Pastoral and *Idyl* sculptures, ca. 1935. Originally flanking the reflecting pool in the center of the Palm House, Lorado Taft's sculptures helped frame the view into the Fern Room.

Taft described these "little whimsies" as "care-free maidens and faun-like youths of some remote period as they might idle and play in the forests of Arcadia."[18] He said:

> "It was my thought merely to make something graceful and appropriate for the greenhouse, something that would add to the impression of fairyland which strikes all visitors in that wonderful place."[19]

The ethereal effect was made all the more dramatic by more than one hundred varieties of orchids displayed near the sculptures.

AUGUST KOCH BRINGS NEW LIFE

In 1912, the West Park Commissioners hired August Koch (1873–1946) as chief horticulturalist. Born in Alsace-Lorraine, Koch studied horticulture at the University of Strasbourg. After immigrating to the United States in 1898, he worked at the internationally respected Missouri Botanical Gardens. Koch brought new life to the Garfield Park Conservatory. He made it a world-class center for botanical research and education while also heightening the beauty that attracted the general public.

Koch improved the collections by replacing duplicate specimens with much rarer ones. He and his staff obtained cuttings, spores, and seeds from various sources. A returning

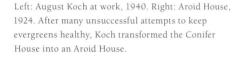

Left: August Koch at work, 1940. Right: Aroid House, 1924. After many unsuccessful attempts to keep evergreens healthy, Koch transformed the Conifer House into an Aroid House.

missionary from Africa brought back a handful of mixed seed that the staff nurtured into magnificent Calatheas. The horticulturalists grew other rare species "from bits of root or spores or seeds that were contained in the packing material around palms and other specimens shipped in from tropical countries."[20] These rare plants enhanced the collection in each room. In the Stove House, the staff added a magnificent vine. This plant, known as the *Vitis lindeni*, suspended its long aerial roots from the rafters to the floor, "forming living curtains across the house to complete the picture of tropical luxuriance."[21]

CONVERTING ROOMS

By 1917, Koch eliminated the New Holland House and moved the Economic House into that room. (Today this is the location of the Elizabeth Morse Genius Children's Garden). He converted the former Economic House into the Bay House, a cool room for storing outdoor plants. Myrtles, oleanders, and other flowering specimens stored there during the winter were moved outdoors in the spring to beautify garden shelters and field houses. In summertime, when the Bay House was empty, the adjacent Economic House plants spilled into this room. The Bay House's growing conditions were so good that in 1928, Koch converted it into a Succulent House, which soon became known as the Desert House.

In the Conifer House, also called the Cold Room, the staff had difficulty keeping its temperature low enough for evergreens. After repeated problems with the collection, Koch made this space into an Aroid House in 1923. Tropical and sub-tropical plants with unusual flowers such as Anthurium, calla lily, and peace lily were featured in the Aroid House. In a manner respectful of Jensen's philosophies, Koch retained the room's original lagoon and stonework, brick paths and edging. Using materials such as traveler's tree, royal elephant's ear, and jack-in-the-pulpit, he layered the plantings and created views as Jensen had done.

EXPANDING THE CONSERVATORY'S ROLE

Koch expanded the Garfield Park Conservatory's educational mission. In 1915, his staff planted "school gardens" in Humboldt, Douglas, and Garfield parks to teach the public the best practices for vegetable gardening. Garfield Park's large school garden was just south of the conservatory. During World War I, the gardens took on special significance because people needed to grow their own food to make up for wartime shortages. As co-sponsor of Garfield Park's war garden, the *Chicago Tribune* published articles to boost public involvement.

Garfield Park Trial Garden, 1921. Originally planted in 1915, gardens of this type were likely inspired by Jensen, who just a few years earlier, had included garden plots for children in his original plans for nearby small parks. First called school gardens, they were later known as trial gardens.

After the war, the gardens remained as demonstration or trial gardens. They displayed layouts and plantings "using the greatest possible variety of useful plant material—both native and exotic—suited to this locality."[22] The Garfield Park Conservatory cooperated with universities by allowing professors to test new plants in these gardens. The gardeners also experimented to see how different varieties of flowers and other plants would thrive in the smoky conditions of Chicago.

Other activities enlightened the public about horticulture. In 1925, the staff began labeling hundreds of plants for the first time. They disseminated free guidebooks about the conservatory and its collections. They provided lectures and demonstrations and began to broadcast a weekly radio program. At flower shows, visitors were encouraged to bring in their own plants for expert identification. Education had become so important that in 1931 the Board of Commissioners added the Museum of Botany to the Garfield Park Conservatory's name.

A MAGICIAN WITH FLOWERS

This page: Small child among the flowers, 1915.
Opposite page: Woman at *Spring Flower Show,* 1929.

For all of his contributions, Koch was most appreciated as the "Magician of Flowers."[23] His impressive displays attracted increasing crowds. As the conservatory's annual attendance swelled from less than 200,000 in 1913 to more than 500,000 in 1927, it was obvious that the facilities needed to expand. The following year, the West Park Commission built a major new exhibition hall with four adjoining propagating houses. This allowed plants to be carted from the propagating houses into the conservatory without exposure to the outdoors, which had long been a problem. The Horticulture Hall addition provided an expansive display house for larger flower shows and events for garden clubs, plant societies, and the general public.

The conservatory's beautiful flower shows drew international acclaim. Koch achieved stunning effects through his masterful use of color and foliage. He said:

> "I never make a plan on paper, I imagine it. Then I change and blend the colors afterwards. I grow the colors for balance. For so many scarlet tulips I grow so many orange calendulas, to tone them down, to balance them...Take the scarlet tulips in Horticulture Hall. Massed together they are vivid scarlet. Put a few of these—scattered in the middle of the purple cineraria. Suddenly purple flashed out in the tulips; and they live."[24]

Top: Water lilies in Garfield Park, ca. 1940. Bottom left: Garden club examining water lily, ca. 1938. Bottom right: Chief Horticulturalist William Blaesing showing plants to two women, ca. 1945.

Instead of the typical colors of white, yellow, and pink for the fall *Chrysanthemum Show*, Koch hybridized hundreds of new varieties in strong autumn shades—corals, oranges, bronzes, and deep reds. He also propagated new mums with unusual petal shapes, textures, and sizes such as a variety with petals that looked like a goose's quill. Groomed to become quite large, some plants were loaded with more than five hundred blossoms and measured seven feet in diameter.

Between the three annual floral exhibits, Koch began changing displays every month. For instance, January emphasized primroses and begonias while May highlighted Martha Washington geraniums, delphiniums, and irises.

Koch and his staff also played an active role in outside activities including Chicago's *Annual Garden and Flower Show*, often held downtown at the Sherman Hotel. They also created displays for the *Horticultural Exhibition* at *A Century of Progress*, Chicago's second world's fair, which was held in 1933 and 1934.

Margaret Kelly at *Chrysanthemum Show*, 1935. Mrs. Kelly was the wife of Edward J. Kelly, who served as mayor of Chicago from 1933 to 1947.

CONTINUING AFTER CONSOLIDATION

In 1934, the newly consolidated Chicago Park District appointed August Koch as chief horticulturalist for the entire system. He supervised a staff of ninety-eight employees responsible for all of the flowers and shrubs throughout the parks and boulevards. Koch brought many of the Garfield Park Conservatory's innovative practices to the other large conservatories at Lincoln and Washington parks. The improvements were short-lived at the Washington Park Conservatory where structural problems soon led to its demolition.

The Chicago Park District's aggressive propagating program resulted in interesting specimens such as the Hippecoris, a cross between the Amaryllis and Lycoris. The floral section became especially famous for its prolific new water lily cultivars. More than fifty different varieties floated in the park lagoons. Among the most popular was the August Koch water lily—an unusual wisteria blue, still in horticultural production today. Other new hybrids were named the Jane Addams, the Pink Pearl, and the Chicago.

A few years after Koch retired in 1940, his protégé William C. Blaesing was appointed chief horticulturalist. Having trained in Germany, Blaesing had worked in Jens Jensen's private office and later as a gardener in Lincoln Park. He served as Koch's assistant at the time of consolidation and continued working for the Chicago Park District until his own retirement twenty-five years later.

WORKING COOPERATIVELY

By working cooperatively with outside groups and individuals, the Park District's horticultural staff continued to enhance the conservatory. To increase their collection of rare and valuable plants, the staff accepted donations of seeds, cuttings, and plants. Botanists at the Field Museum of Natural History contributed seeds of palms obtained during expeditions to Guatemala, Brazil, and Trinidad. The museum's staff also donated hundreds of species of orchids, bromeliads, cacti, aroids, and other tropical plants. Important gifts came from individuals including a former explorer who brought back plants from Columbia, Peru, and Ecuador. A private donor gave dozens of Euphorbias, a varied group of succulents planted in the Desert House. On September 20, 1940, the room stayed open until midnight so that the public could view several night-blooming cacti that flowered with four hundred individual blooms.

Garden clubs and flower societies staged their own shows in Horticulture Hall with assistance from the staff. The Hawthorne Garden Club, made up entirely of Western Electric Company employees, held two annual flower shows. Other exhibits focusing on individual species were sponsored by the Delphinium Society, Central States Dahlia Society, and the Midwest Horticulture Society, which hosted an annual Iris exhibition.

Left: Garden club competition in Horticulture Hall, c. 1940. Right: Cactus room, ca. 1949. David Alverez and other conservatory staff members were photographed while planting a cactus that was donated from the Chicago Railroad Fair.

HIGH STANDARDS DURING WWII

Despite the labor shortages caused by World War II, the horticultural staff maintained its high standards for the conservatories and gardens. Women helped to fill the void caused by men leaving for war. These new recruits, like millions of other American women who joined the labor force during the war, were often referred to as "Rosie the Riveter." Instead of serving as factory workers, in Garfield Park, women worked as laborers and staff florists.

The Chicago Park District also played an active role in promoting Victory Gardens which helped offset food shortages and provided a patriotic activity for civilians. The horticulturalists gave demonstrations in war gardens in several parks, including one adjacent to the Garfield Park Conservatory. They also helped with other Victory Gardens throughout the city. This community outreach was especially valuable as the distraction of the war kept many Chicagoans from visiting the conservatories.

To revive flagging attendance during the wartime, the Garfield Park Conservatory added a major *Azalea Show*. Opening in February of 1943, it showcased more than forty-five varieties of azaleas and some rhododendrons. It was so well received that the following year, the *Azalea Show* became the fourth seasonal flower show at both the Lincoln and Garfield Park conservatories. This practice has continued annually to the present day.

Left: Actress Celeste Holm at preview of the
Chrysanthemum Show, 1949. Right: Couple
enjoying the chrysanthemums, 1953.

POST-WAR PROGRESS

As World War II drew to a close in the fall of 1945, the two conservatories enjoyed renewed popularity. With peacetime came greater media attention. Colonel Robert R. McCormick, editor and publisher of the *Chicago Tribune* was so impressed by the 1946 *Azalea Show* at the Garfield Park Conservatory that he sent a writer to prepare a lengthy feature article describing the display. Attendance soared in response to the coverage.

Two years later during the *Chrysanthemum Show*, an even more enticing newspaper article resulted in the highest single-day attendance of both conservatories—purportedly 44,754 at Garfield, and 11,717 at Lincoln. It raved:

> "Right now a wonderland of color is abloom in both of these glassed-in gardens, 13,000 chrysanthemums of all shades and more than 600 varieties…This is the nation's biggest mum show, a triumph of horticultural research and artistry." [25]

Besides the seasonal flower shows, the valuable and alluring orchid collections were a major attraction all year long. The Garfield Park Conservatory had the largest and most varied orchid collection in the city, with a display that changed weekly. Its entire stock was grown in Kilbourn Park, while the Lincoln Park Conservatory produced all of its own orchids. Although Kilbourn Park's greenhouse was entirely devoted to orchid production, two other small greenhouses in Marquette and Indian Boundary parks propagated perennials and annuals for many lush and beautiful gardens throughout the city.

"I don't remember what year of high school it was, we had to put a book together of different leaves. So I remember walking to the conservatory, taking leaves, and putting the book together with all the exotic Latin names that were on all of the signage in the conservatory, being very proud of my effort. I got an 'F,' failing because what I had done was inappropriate. I should not have picked the leaves at the conservatory, so that was the essence, and rightly so."

—Diane Kelley

Fern Room, 1912.

The Chicago Park District's publicity department launched a "Flower of the Month" program in 1949. On the first day of each month, daily newspapers would highlight the featured plant, which was then displayed prominently at the conservatories. When celebrities such as singer Kitty Kallen and actresses Celeste Holm and Mary Meade appeared in Chicago, they often posed with the "Flower of the Month." Along with newspaper and radio coverage, plant-related stories began appearing on the new local television stations. The media attention helped increase attendance at both conservatories to a combined total that exceeded two million in 1950.

LEAKY-ROOF FAIRYLAND

Structures made of glass are especially difficult to maintain, and after forty years, the Garfield Park Conservatory was deteriorating. A newspaper article entitled "Leaky-Roof Fairyland" reported that a visit to the conservatory "is not without pain to those who remember it, only a few years ago, as one of the outstanding institutions in the city."[26] It specifically described the damaged plants in the leaky Economic House. Luckily, the house soon received major structural repairs that included completely reglazing the roof. After damaged specimens were replaced, the room's collection of useful plants reopened to the public in October of 1948.

The rehabilitation of other rooms soon followed. After the Aroid House was renovated in 1950, the staff began emptying out over a thousand cacti and other succulents from the

Left: Aroid House renovation, ca. 1950. Right: Fern Room renovation, ca. 1952. All of the plants in the Fern Room had to be removed for their protection.

Desert House to prepare for its reconstruction. Horticulturalist Robert T. Van Tress went on a six-week collecting expedition through New Mexico and Arizona to obtain new cacti for the restored room.

Beginning in 1952, Park District forces undertook major repairs to the Fern Room. Its entire collection, including the ancient cycads, was removed and stored temporarily in the Lincoln Park Conservatory's Fern Room, which had been rehabilitated the previous year. After the two-year construction project, Garfield Park Conservatory's lush Fern Room quickly recovered to look as though it had never been touched.

REPAIRING AND RECONSTRUCTING

To address the problems of cracked and broken glass that were plaguing the entire Garfield Park Conservatory, the Chicago Park District began a series of repair and reconstruction projects throughout the other five rooms. Park District architects were determined to find a modern solution. In remodeling Horticulture Hall in 1956, they called for the removal of all of the glass and its replacement with fiberglass panels.

The next year, the staff began analyzing the terrible problems with the Palm House structure. The failure of its original steel trusses caused continual glass breakage and its entry vestibule was small and cramped. After completely demolishing the structure, including the vestibule, the Park District constructed an entirely new Palm House of aluminum and

Left: Demolition of the original Palm House, 1958. Right: Florida Palms being replanted after reconstruction of Palm House, 1961.

fiberglass. It had a larger entry pavilion with bathrooms, offices, and a more expansive lobby. Completed in 1958, the $540,000 project involved removing and storing three thousand plants. Some of the palms weighed more than one ton.

Although the architects generally followed the Palm House's original dimensions, they did not fully replicate its gentle form nor did they save any interior details. The structure's "elegant lacy truss system" was instead "replaced with a bolder structure of I-beam construction."[27] The International Modern style of the new pavilion and its opaque fiberglass sheathing also gave the building a heavy and foreboding appearance.

Due to damage from ultraviolet light, the fiberglass panels had to be frequently recoated and replaced. Fortunately, the experiments with fiberglass did not extend to other rooms. When the Park District renovated the Warm House in 1963 and the Show House in 1967, glass was chosen. Despite the upheaval caused by so many construction projects, the conservatory hosted its four annual flower shows throughout the period.

GROWING AND PLANTING IN OLD AND NEW WAYS

In the 1960s, propagating and planting continued in old and new ways. Between the two large conservatories and the three smaller greenhouses, the horticulturalists grew over a half million plants annually. The Garfield Park Conservatory's staff continued

Left: Garden for the Blind, ca. 1970. This is now called the Sensory Garden. Right: Mayor Richard J. Daley and his wife Eleanor at a preview of the *Chrysanthemum Show*, 1963. Mrs. Eleanor Daley was presented with a mum named in her honor.

establishing and naming new hybrids that were often presented in special ceremonies. In 1963, new chrysanthemums were named the "Eleanor Daley," honoring Mayor Richard J. Daley's wife; and the "WBKB-ABC," for a television station that often featured the conservatory. The following year, the Chicago Park District presented the "Karyn Kupcinet" Amarylis to *Sun-Times* Columnist Irv Kupcinet and his wife Essee, as a memorial to their daughter, a Hollywood actress who was mysteriously murdered.

Propagating unusual plants often required great perseverance. On a trip with his wife in 1960, horticulturalist Robert Van Tress acquired a rare double coconut palm seed from the Royal Botanical Garden in Ceylon.[28] The plant, *Lodoicea maldivica*, produces an extremely large seed that is exceptionally difficult to grow in a greenhouse. Van Tress fervently hoped to cultivate it, but his attempt failed. After Van Tress retired in 1967, his colleagues remained committed to cultivating the rare plant. Purchasing another double coconut seed for twenty-five dollars, the "staff had to dig a six-foot silo and line it with lead coil to maintain the 80-degree temperature necessary for the seed to grow."[29] Although its chances for survival seemed minimal, the double coconut thrived and remains one of the most important plants in the collections today.

In 1970, the Sensory Garden was created on the conservatory grounds. Inspired by precedents in Europe, this garden had vegetables, herbs, and native flowers that could be touched and smelled. It was originally named the Garden for the Blind. The garden, with low walls to help guide people through the space, continues to delight visitors.

Girls with Easter Baskets promoting "Flower of the Month," ca. 1970.

CHANGING TIMES

The Garfield Park Conservatory's standards declined significantly throughout the 1970s and 1980s, partly as a result of larger problems within the Chicago Park District. Citizens throughout Chicago "complained that a political patronage system produced an incompetent park work force," and that "parks in minority neighborhoods" were especially neglected.[30] Civic groups filed a complaint with the U.S. Justice Department in 1982, which was settled through a consent decree. It took several more years, however, before reform efforts had a noticeable effect on the conservatory.

As negative perceptions of the neighborhood began to affect attendance at the Garfield Park Conservatory, the smaller facility in Lincoln Park became more popular. In 1971, the combined attendance of the two conservatories was about the same as it had been for the previous twenty years. But now, the Lincoln Park Conservatory had more than 1.6 million

Left: *Easter Show*, 1969. Right: Palm House after reconstruction with fiberglass sheathing, ca. 1970.

visitors—nearly twice the attendance of the Garfield Park Conservatory. By the 1980s, as Park District deficiencies grew more troubling, attendance plummeted in both facilities, especially at Garfield Park.

The flower shows, long known for their artistry, had become kitschy and poorly designed. A 1984 *Chicago Tribune* article described the Easter shows. It touted, "Each will have a life-size cross made out of blossoms and a non-floral Easter attraction: live rabbits in Garfield Park and mechanical gnomes coloring eggs in Lincoln Park."[31] Similarly, the Christmas shows had potted poinsettias forming giant trees and flocking on real trees. The flower shows had long been created through a careful collaboration between a landscape designer and the horticulturalists resulting in a cohesive composition. Now, they were the result of various staff members who were each given their own plot in the Show House and Horticulture Hall.

The atmosphere at the conservatories had become especially difficult for well-trained and hard-working staff members. They had to co-exist with unscrupulous employees who stole plants or idled away time without working. While politically connected individuals filled valuable positions, the remaining staff still had to grow tens of thousands of plants, produce four annual flower shows, and give hundreds of guided tours each year.

THE TURN-AROUND BEGINS

The election of Mayor Richard M. Daley in 1989 marked a new era in the greening and rehabilitation of Chicago's parks. Rumors that the Chicago Park District had plans to close down the Garfield Park Conservatory quickly spread, particularly after dozens of laborers and florists were laid off. Efforts had quietly begun, however, to turn the facility around. The conservatory desperately needed help. Annual attendance had reached an all-time low, well under 50,000, and the aged facility was deteriorating. In 1993, the Park District's Engineering Department hired John Eifler, a preservation architect, to assess the entire structure. He identified the restoration of the Fern Room as the highest priority and began working on the project.

A disastrous incident soon shifted the focus. In January of 1994, the conservatory staff received a warning that Chicago would soon experience a record cold snap. To protect the cycads and other rare plants, the staff wrapped them in plastic sheeting and borrowed kerosene-burning heaters from Soldier Field to keep the plants warm. But the steam pipes burst and the indoor temperature plunged to a disastrous twenty-five degrees. As a result, a large percentage of the Aroid House's exotic plants were killed or badly injured.[32]

After the Park District authorized funding for emergency repairs to the Aroid House, the Garfield Park Advisory Council and other neighborhood groups strongly advocated for the restoration of the entire conservatory. Park District officials called together a task force of many concerned organizations. The Friends of the Parks, a nonprofit advocacy group, led the task force that developed a vision for a restored conservatory with new programs that would attract large numbers of people and serve the surrounding community.

Arbor Day, 1990. To draw attention to the Garfield Park Conservatory which was then considered its "hidden oasis," the Chicago Park District held the 35th *Annual Arbor Day and Environmental Celebration* there.

Left: Labyrinth, 2006. Installed next to the Sensory Garden in the late 1990s, this labyrinth was the gift of Posy Kriebahl. Right: Tour of conservatory improvements, 2000. Depicted from left to right are Director of Conservatories Lisa Roberts, Alderman Ed Smith, Mayor Richard M. Daley, and Chicago Park District General Superintendent David Doig.

An urban parks initiative sponsored by the Lila Wallace-Reader's Digest Foundation provided a $1.46 million challenge grant fostering the creation of a new organization, the Garfield Park Conservatory Alliance. This nonprofit group would partner with the Chicago Park District to bring new life to the conservatory. The matching grant was co-funded by the Park District, other donors, and foundations.

While the Alliance began taking over the public dimension of the conservatory including education, visitor services, and programming, the Park District continued to restore the structure. Responding to widespread news coverage about the freeze, large donations came in from businesses and individuals who wanted to help. A new long-range plan to fully rehabilitate the conservatory was developed. In the fall of 1994, Mayor Daley and Chicago Park District Superintendent Forrest Claypool announced that at least eight million dollars would be committed to physical improvements over the next eight years.

AMBITIOUS PLANS TAKE ROOT

The reopening of the Aroid House in 1995 marked a new era at the conservatory. The restored room looked exactly as it did in the 1920s. Its trusses, glazing, mechanical systems, lagoon, and brick paths were meticulously restored. Horticulturalist John Raffetto carefully selected the new plants based on historic photographs and plant lists.

With the Alliance taking over most of the educational responsibilities, the Park District began a major restructuring that included the creation of several professional positions such as director of conservatories and curator of plants. In partnership with the Alliance, the new professional staff members would help to return the conservatory to its earlier level of excellence. Park District architects and landscape architects coordinated the numerous restoration projects that followed.

Despite some growing pains, progress was soon visible. The Parkways Foundation, another nonprofit partner, orchestrated a major fundraising campaign to help the conservatory attract an underserved audience: families with children. Along with other donations, a major gift from the Elizabeth Morse Genius Charitable Trust supported the transformation of the aging Economic House into an educational and interactive Children's Garden.

In the late 1990s, two major construction projects improved visitor services by adding unprecedented opportunities for programming. At Horticulture Hall, glass replaced the fiberglass panels and the space was redesigned to accommodate weddings, meetings, special events, and the on-going flower shows. The Park District also tore down the 1950s entry pavilion and replaced it with a structure designed by Booth Hansen Associates. With a gift shop, community room, and classrooms, the addition provided vibrant new spaces. Federal Empowerment Zone funds supported these construction projects because of their relevance not only to the conservatory, but also to community revitalization.

Left: Horticulture Hall, 2007. Right: Activities in the Elizabeth Morse Genius Children's Garden, 2006. The Garfield Park Conservatory Alliance has provided special programs for children and families since the late 1990s.

"If you feel that your current area isn't safe, you can always go to the conservatory. Also, the conservatory has many free events that I love to attend… [It provides] a great learning experience for both adults and children. Such events include *County Fair*, *Creatures of the Night*, *Chocolate Fest*, and many more."

—Latrice T., Green Teen, age 17

"The Garfield Park Conservatory provides a place where the whole family can come and relax. There is a place for the children to come…called the Childen's Garden. While the children are in the garden the parents can be enjoying the different rooms here in the conservatory."

—Tanika, age 17

Elizabeth Morse Genius Children's Garden, 2006.

CULTIVATING IMPROVEMENTS AND PROGRAMS

At the turn of the twenty-first century, the partnership between the Chicago Park District
and Garfield Park Conservatory Alliance cultivated further improvements and programs.
The Warm House, which has some of the only flowering cocoa trees in Chicago, became the
Sweet House that features plants used in confections and desserts, such as chocolate, sugar
cane, chewing gum, and cinnamon.

In 2000, this new focus inspired an enticing event, *Chocolate Fest*, which attracted huge
crowds to the conservatory for the first time in years. "The highlight came when collections
curator Thomas Antonio mounted a step ladder, plucked a softball-sized pod from a chocolate tree and cracked it open with a machete to reveal a few dozen cocoa beans."[33] While
showing the beans, Antonio explained how chocolate is made.

The event has continued every year on the weekend before Valentine's Day. "The Annual
Chocolate Fest not only gives Chicagoans the chance to sample a variety of chocolate, it
gives them the option to learn about the plant origins of this favorite food," said Timothy
J. Mitchell, General Superintendent of the Chicago Park District.[34]

Continuing the new momentum, the Garfield Park Conservatory opened a *Pink Flamingo
Flower Show* in the spring of 2000. The Alliance sponsored related family workshops, scav-
enger hunts, and plant clinics. In the spirit of the trial gardens that historically flourished
next to the conservatory, the Alliance planted a Demonstration Garden to teach people
about community and organic gardening. Covering the same amount of space as a regular
city lot, it is divided into areas featuring vegetable and herb gardening, beekeeping, composting, and other techniques used to grow food.

This page, top: Monet Garden just east of Horticulture Hall, 2004. This page, bottom: Dale Chihuly. Opposite page: During the exhibit *A Garden of Glass,* 2001.

Another garden improvement arose from the 2000 *Flower and Garden Show* at Navy Pier. There, the Park District horticulturalists had created an impressive display inspired by the famous painter Claude Monet. After the show, they planted a garden next to Horticulture Hall outside of the conservatory. Like Monet's 's gardens at Giverney, France, it contains sunflowers, nasturtiums, poppies, peonies, irises, and smaller "paint box" flower beds.

During this period, the conservatory's collections and interpretative materials were upgraded. The Park District removed redundant plants and added rarer ones. Desert plants from the Lincoln Park Conservatory were moved to Garfield, and most of the orchids moved from Garfield to Lincoln to provide more cohesion. The flower shows became more intricate with larger and more diverse palettes of perennials, annuals, bulbs, and shrubs. The traditional *Chrysanthemum Show* became an outdoor *Harvest Festival* with an annual county fair that includes a gardening competition, music, and entertainment.

THE FUTURE IN GLASS

In 2001, a reconstructed "L" stop at North Central Park Avenue and West Lake Street provided much better access to the conservatory. The timing was especially good because that fall the Garfield Park Conservatory hosted a spectacular exhibit featuring the work of renowned artist Dale Chihuly. This event restored the Garfield Park Conservatory to Chicago's cultural forefront. It was "a true urban miracle — glass flowers hidden in beds... glass lily pads sprouting in ponds," and glass reeds blooming among cacti.[35] The exhibition drew so much attention that it was extended twice — and remained for almost a year.

Lisa Roberts, the Chicago Park District Director of Conservatories at that time, said:

> "I anticipated this was going to be popular, but I didn't anticipate it was going to be as magical as it turned out to be... People say they're looking at the artwork with new eyes, to see it in a setting so essentially organic... Especially at night, it's unbelievable. People walk in and gasp." [36]

Chihuly in the Park: A Garden of Glass attracted an unprecedented level of national media attention including the Today Show and CNN. By the time it closed at the end of 2002, more than 575,000 people had visited. Most had never been to the conservatory before. Several Chicago businessmen were so enthralled with the exhibit that they raised hundreds of thousands of dollars to permanently acquire several of Chihuly's yellow lily pads for the Aroid House.

CONTAGIOUS SUCCESS

Other successes were prompted by *Chihuly in the Park: A Garden of Glass*. Befittingly, public donations collected during the glass exhibit went towards the reglazing of the Palm House. The project included the dramatic replacement of the 1950s fiberglass panels with glass, along with new environmental controls, including automatic heating, venting, shading, and misting systems.

As with many earlier renovations, this one required the removal of most of the plants from the Palm House prior to construction. Moving the large and rare palms presented an arduous task. The staff was most worried about the survival of the double coconut which has been described as the "Mona Lisa of palms." [37] Because Garfield Park's tree is the largest double coconut palm "growing in captivity in the world," the horticulturalists believed that it was "the single most important plant we'll ever move." [38] Forty years after it was first planted, the palm's leaves were pressing against the curved roof in a corner of the Palm House. After the reglazing project, laborers carefully replanted it in the center area providing the room's full height. Much to everyone's relief, the conservatory's "Mona Lisa" is thriving.

Left: Reglazing the Palm House, 2003. Right: Replanting palms after the reglazing project, 2003.

A Garden of Glass, inspired a larger vision for special exhibits and displays. In 2003, the Garfield Park Conservatory Alliance and the Chicago Botanic Garden collaboratively sponsored *Chapungu: Custom & Legend, A Culture in Stone*, which featured contemporary sculptures from Zimbabwe. The exhibition was divided between the Chicago and Glencoe locations. The following year, Project Exploration, a nonprofit science education organization, hosted *Giants: African Dinosaurs* at the conservatory. Highlighting the discoveries of world-famous paleontologist Paul Sereno and his wife, educator Gabrielle Lyon, the exhibit placed full-scale replicas of dinosaurs into realistic settings amidst the lush vegetation.

BEYOND THE GLASS WALLS

In recent years, the role of the conservatory has been broadened to extend well beyond its glass walls. Planning initiatives that began in 2002 called for extending the conservatory's campus to the north and west. Non-public areas of Garfield Park will be converted into facilities that support the community and help the conservatory become a major center of horticulture in the Midwest.

The Chicago Park District began these efforts by converting the maintenance yard north of the conservatory into the Garfield Park Market Place. The next phase focused on transforming a Jenney-designed stable building into an education center. As plans were progressing in 2003, the stable burned to the ground.

Undeterred by the disastrous fire, other aspects of the plan continued moving forward. The City Garden was created in underutilized spaces next to the conservatory. While gardens often provide a refuge from urban life, this one embraces it by featuring urban hardy vegetation, plant "communities," and interesting recycled materials. Its undulating and free-flowing beds are quite unlike the traditional "outdoor rooms" of other botanic gardens. Douglas Hoerr designed the garden in collaboration with Park District landscape architect Robert J. Megquier and horticulturalist Adam Schwerner. The City Garden's second phase was realized in 2007.

The Alliance and the Park District are developing new plans calling for the transformation of the additional park maintenance yards, shops, and buildings into a much larger conservatory campus. The expanded campus will include more classrooms, lecture and meeting rooms, resource and volunteer centers, staff offices, artists' studios, a café, and modernized production green houses. The Garfield Park Market Place will be enlarged with spaces for farmer's markets, gardening demonstrations, outdoor dining, and summer concerts.

Left: Educational program for *Chapungu: Custom & Legend*, 2003. Right: *Giants: African Dinosaurs* at the Garfield Park Conservatory, 2004.

HANDS-ON LEARNING

As it reaches its second century, the Garfield Park Conservatory is achieving its mission to educate the public about plants and gardening in compelling and engaging ways. Classes on beekeeping, composting, and hands-on gardening are offered regularly in the demonstration gardens. Weekend plant clinics are given at the conservatory in conjunction with the University of Illinois Extension. Guided tree identification walks use the entire park as a textbook.

Addressing the widespread void in public education about plants and their critical role in our survival, the Alliance and the Park District recently developed an interactive exhibit called *Sugar from the Sun*. Funded in part by a grant from the National Science Foundation, this $4.75 million permanent exhibit uses plants, air, water, and sunlight to interpret the building blocks and product of photosynthesis. Located in the former Sweet House, the new exhibit shows how plants sustain all life on earth with their ability to make food with sunlight energy.

MORE THAN HORTICULTURE

Left: Garfield Market Place, 2005. Artists and other vendors use converted horse sheds to sell their wares. Right: Plant identification walk sponsored by the Alliance, 2007.

The Garfield Park Conservatory has become much more than a horticultural center. "People know that plants have power of some kind…There is something transformative about stepping into this place. Conservatories around the world are experiencing a rebirth now

Left: "Nikigator," 2007. Right: "Guardian Lion," 2007. Niki de Saint Phalle's playful sculptures enlivened the conservatory between the spring and late fall of 2007.

because people appreciate what they can do for the soul,"[39] said Adam Schwerner, Chicago Park District Director of Natural Resources.

Recognizing the uplifting qualities of art as well as nature, the conservatory has become a mecca for cultural programming and art exhibits. In 2007, large whimsical sculptures by the internationally-acclaimed artist Niki de Saint Phalle filled the conservatory and its grounds. *Niki in the Garden* featured more than thirty monumental and playful fiberglass artworks embellished with mirrors, glass, and ceramic mosaics. The exhibit was fun for children because many of the brightly colored sculptures invited climbing. Among the special programs were *Niki Nights*, which featured dance, music, and poetry.

A CENTURY MILESTONE

Reaching its century milestone in 2008, the conservatory has once again become a valuable asset to the City of Chicago. Annual attendance has soared to nearly 200,000 as city residents and tourists continue to discover this remarkable place.

In celebration, the Chicago Park District and the Garfield Park Conservatory Alliance are hosting many parties and festivals, concert series, and exhibits. Oral histories of local residents have been recorded, and school children have written about their experiences as members of the Garfield Park community. These events honor the conservatory's past and also celebrate a living, growing, and evolving future. ❖

"The building itself, what was in it, especially the Fern Room, was a different world."

—Marley Sackheim

"I lost my father at the age of 49, and eight years later my mother found out she had incurable cancer. The day she was diagnosed I went straight to the Fern Room. It's a place that really embraces you. The Garfield Park Conservatory was the only place where I could find solace — a respite when I really needed it."

—Michael W. Scott

Fern Room, 2005.

"If you come to Garfield Park, I promise you will have fun."

—Jarrod M., Willa Cather Elementary School

"I was 12 years old. The day started out when I woke up. It was hot outside. I looked at the news and it said it was feelin' good outside. I woke my brother up to get the day started. We did what we had to do and called our friends. My friends asked, 'What are we going to do?' We all said 'Go to Garfield Park!'"

—Charles P., Willa Cather Elementary School

Dancers at *Harvest Fest*, 2001.

THE COMMUNITY

MORE THAN A CENTURY AGO, ideas and visions of nature helped shape the West Side into one of Chicago's most interesting neighborhoods. A seminal park and boulevard system gave the area lovely green spaces and spurred the construction of fine architecture. In the mid-twentieth century, the neighborhood underwent struggle, poverty, and change. Today, dedicated citizens are using the gardening and greening movement as a catalyst for reviving this vital part of Chicago.

Boulevard entrance into Garfield Park, ca. 1910.

FAR WEST SIDE

During Chicago's early history, a fashionable neighborhood along North and South Ashland Avenue was considered the Far West Side. Wealthy citizens chose to settle there for several reasons. The neighborhood sat on high ground, far away from the stench of the raw sewage dumped into the Chicago River. Relatively close to the city's early commercial district on West Lake Street, it had good transportation via horse trolleys, hansom cabs, and other carriages. Prominent residents lived in the area's elegant mansions and rowhouses such as Mayor Carter Harrison; famous entertainment impresario Florenz Ziegfeld; and Mary Todd Lincoln, who settled there shortly after the assassination of her husband, President Abraham Lincoln.

By the early 1860s, the Far West Side had two other attractions, Union and Jefferson parks. Although they were lovely green spaces, the two small parks could not meet the needs of the growing community. West Siders pushed for a more substantial park system. Citizens helped draft a bill to create an ambitious park and boulevard system that would promote the development of fine residential neighborhoods throughout the area. Approved by the State in 1869, the legislation annexed a large undeveloped area, moving Chicago's western boundary from Western Avenue to what is now Pulaski Road. The newly appointed West Park Commissioners identified specific sites to be acquired and transformed into three large parks eventually named Humboldt, Garfield, and Douglas parks. The commissioners were also mandated to create a ribbon of landscaped boulevards that would connect these parks and link them to the South and Lincoln Park systems.

EFFECTS OF THE CHICAGO FIRE

On October 8, 1871, a fire that started in a barn at West Dekoven and South Jefferson streets raged into a catastrophic inferno. Its origin was less than two miles from the West Park District, but because the Chicago River acted as buffer, this region was protected from the flames. Although the settled West Side did not burn, the Great Chicago Fire had a major impact there. Throngs of Chicagoans made homeless by the fire crowded into the area. As these newcomers built homes, shops, and factories, older residents began moving out.

After the fire, upper-middle-class families built row houses and single-family homes in the Italianate and Second Empire styles. Examples of these elegant structures of brick and Joliet limestone remain along West Monroe and West Adams streets, as well as West Jackson and West Washington boulevards. The Union Park Congregational Church (now First Baptist

Opposite page, top: Ashland Avenue from Adams Street, Washington Boulevard, and Ogden Avenue, ca. 1900. Bottom left: Funeral Procession, 1893. Huge crowds gathered in front of Mayor Carter Harrison, Sr.'s home on North Ashland Avenue after his assassination. Bottom right: West Jackson Boulevard east from South Paulina Street, 1896.

Devastation in the wake of the Great Chicago Fire, 1871.
Opposite page: Map of the West Side, 2007.

Congregational Church) is a vestige from this era. Today, this neighborhood is known as the Near West Side or West Haven.

The Great Chicago Fire also spurred development southwest into North Lawndale. Speculators Millard & Decker had recently subdivided this area. To attract good housing and give the neighborhood a more verdant appeal, they named it "Lawndale." McCormick Reaper Works built a factory just east of North Lawndale, at the southeast corner of South Western and South Blue Island avenues, after the fire destroyed its old complex. Plant workers flocked to nearby blocks and built modest frame houses and cottages.

GROWTH RADIATING TO THE WEST

The area north of Lawndale and west of the settled Near West Side was slower to develop. Even after the West Park Bill spurred an initial flurry of land speculation, little construction occurred east of Garfield Park. To provide better access to the site, the West Park Commission improved West Washington Boulevard in 1885. Despite the new boulevard, horse-drawn car lines in this area were among the slowest in the city, and the poor transportation impeded neighborhood growth.

The West Garfield Park community began developing in the early 1870s when the Galena and Chicago Union Railroad (later Chicago & North Western Railway) built its manufacturing shops there. This prompted the settlement of thousands of German, Irish, and

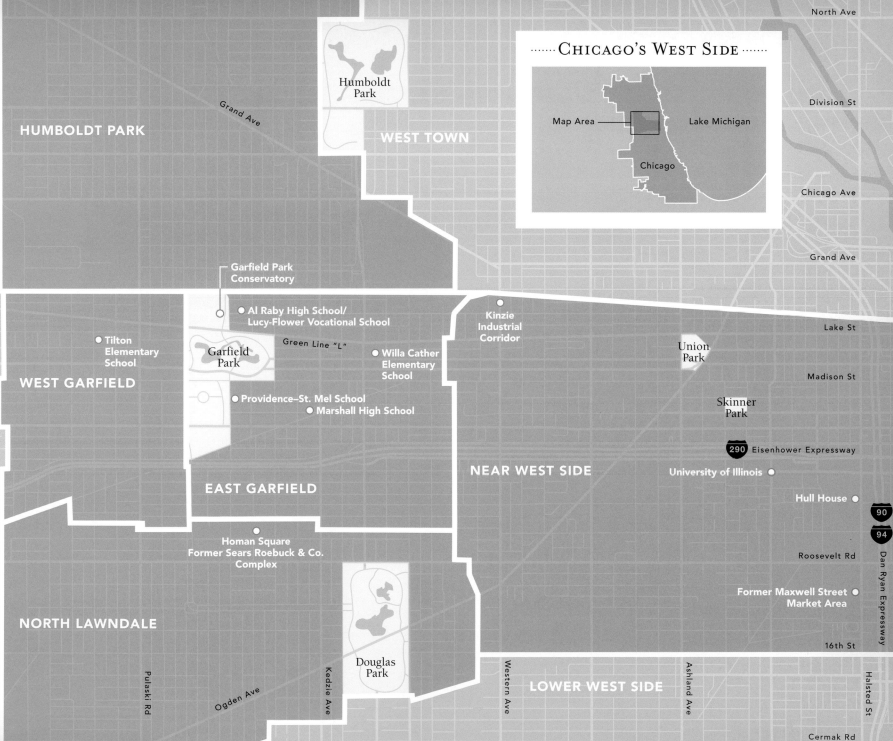

CHICAGO'S WEST SIDE

Map Area
Lake Michigan
Chicago

North Ave
Division St
Chicago Ave
Grand Ave

HUMBOLDT PARK

Humboldt Park

WEST TOWN

Grand Ave

Garfield Park Conservatory

Al Raby High School/
Lucy-Flower Vocational School

Kinzie Industrial Corridor

Lake St

Tilton Elementary School

Green Line "L"

Garfield Park

Willa Cather Elementary School

Union Park

Madison St

WEST GARFIELD

Providence–St. Mel School

Marshall High School

Skinner Park

290 Eisenhower Expressway

EAST GARFIELD

NEAR WEST SIDE

University of Illinois

Hull House

90

Homan Square
Former Sears Roebuck & Co.
Complex

94

NORTH LAWNDALE

Douglas Park

Roosevelt Rd

Former Maxwell Street
Market Area

16th St

Pulaski Rd

Kedzie Ave

Western Ave

LOWER WEST SIDE

Ashland Ave

Halsted St

Ogden Ave

Cermak Rd

Left: Racing past tower at West Side Club, 1905.
Right: G.W. Kitterman, driver of racehorse Chop Suey on the track at West Side Club, 1905.

Scandinavian workers and their families. These immigrant families built small brick and frame houses. With the new park at the center of the neighborhood, the area was originally named Central Park.

Within a few years, neighborhood growth was bolstered by the West Side Club, also known as the Gentleman's Trotting and Racing Club. Despite its genteel name, the race track attracted beer gardens, saloons, and other seedy businesses to open along West Madison Street. Even honest workers who disapproved of the race track enjoyed watching the handlers exercise the horses on Sundays. Spectators throughout the region came to the club not only for the horse racing, but also for events such as boxing matches, the 1882 Illinois State Fair, and Buffalo Bill's Wild West Show.

WORLD'S COLUMBIAN EXPOSITION SPURS GROWTH

When Chicago won the honor of hosting the *World's Columbian Exposition* in 1890, there was much debate about the best location for the fairgrounds. The West Park Commissioners suggested that their entire system, including all of the parks and connecting boulevards, should become the site of the fair. They thought the vast unimproved spaces in the parks made their offer especially attractive, and West Siders agreed.

By this time, transportation services were much better. Several streetcar lines came into the area. In 1892, the Lake Street Elevated Railway Company formed to build a tracking

Left: Traffic on Lake Street during construction of "L,"
1892. Center: Building the Lake Street "L," 1892.
Right: 4-Track structure being erected, 1892.

structure that ran east-west through Garfield Park. Neighborhood proponents of the fair
estimated that streetcars and the West Side "L" could transport as many as two million
people to and from the proposed West Side exposition each day.

Renowned landscape architect Frederick Law Olmsted studied many possible sites for the
fair and recommended one on the South Side that had Lake Michigan as a backdrop. The
West Side parks were not chosen, and the *World's Columbian Exposition* took place on the
lakefront in Jackson Park in 1893.

VICTORIAN-ERA IMPROVEMENTS

Although the West Side did not host the exposition, the event spurred improvements
throughout the city. On the West Side, development was most intense near the elevated
tracks. Many of the remaining streets and boulevards were paved. As taxes downtown
increased, companies found the West Side a desirable alternative, and factories, warehouses,
and manufacturing plants began springing up.

The 1890s brought a collection of handsome houses, town homes, and apartment buildings
rendered in Classical, Queen Anne, and other Victorian styles. Prolific Chicago architects
such as Otis Wheelock, D.S. Pentecost, and Fromann & Jebsen produced designs using an
eclectic vocabulary of turrets, varied rooflines, metal cornices, and leaded-glass windows.
Thousands of these structures were built of brick faced with Bedford limestone. They are

Left: Lucille Nau, Queen of the *West Madison Street Carnival*, 1904. Right: Neighborhood scene looking west from Kedzie Avenue, ca. 1900.

now considered Chicago Greystones. Other residences were composed of brick in various shades of blonde, brown, and red, often in combination with limestone. Ornamental details in pressed brick and carved stone enlivened the facades.

By the turn of the century, the West Side was an established neighborhood with schools, churches, and businesses. Many shops and restaurants opened along West Madison Street and the area between Western and Crawford avenues became a thriving business district. (Crawford Avenue was later renamed Pulaski Road.)

In 1903, the first electric street lights were installed. Merchants organized a week-long carnival in celebration of the new lights. Extra incandescent lights were "…strung across the street in festoons every 200 feet" with "bunting and Japanese lanterns…to add to the brilliance of the scene."[1] Vacant lots were filled with amusement tents, circuses, and an Indian encampment. Other attractions included a parade of funeral hearses leading a band playing dirges, a "chicken coop on an antiquated wagon and filled with live rooster, which crowed lustily whenever the band played," and two "ancient Roman chariots, one said to contain Ben-Hur and the other Ben-Him."[2] The *West Madison Street Carnival* continued annually for about a decade.

PRAIRIE-INSPIRED DESIGNS

During this period, several progressive Chicago architects and landscape architects developed a uniquely Midwestern design expression. They were inspired by the inherent beauty of the prairie and were also influenced by the organic architecture of Louis Sullivan. The Prairie style of architecture emphasized horizontality, earthy colors, clean lines, and simplicity on a comfortable human scale.

A number of important Prairie School architects had commissions on the city's West Side. Frank Lloyd Wright designed a row of brick apartments for developer Edward C. Waller in 1895. An innovative example of early affordable housing, several of the original structures remain on West Walnut Street near North Francisco Avenue. Architect George Maher designed the King-Nash House with strong horizontal lines and a thistle motif woven throughout its limestone façade. It is still standing on the 3200 block of West Washington Boulevard.

Prairie School architects also created non-residential structures on the West Side. Frank Lloyd Wright designed a factory at 3005 West Carroll Avenue, in the industrial corridor at the north end of the neighborhood. In 1901, Hugh M.G. Garden (subsequently of the firm Schmidt, Garden & Martin) incorporated prairie-inspired elements into a largely Greek Revival composition at the Third Church of Christ, Scientist. The landmark building later became the Metropolitan Missionary Baptist Church. Dwight H. Perkins, who served as

Left: Tilton School looking northwest from West End Avenue, ca. 1908. Right: Columbus Park waterfall, ca. 1925. Jens Jensen designed two waterfalls to serve as symbolic sources of Columbus Park's prairie river.

architect to the Board of Education created a modern structure with strong geometric forms for Tilton School. Located at the corner of North Keeler and West End avenues the building represents a bold departure from traditional school architecture.

In 1905, Sears Roebuck and Company, the "world's largest mail-order company" hired the Prairie School firm of Nimmons & Fellows to design what was then the "world's largest commercial building."[3] The massive fifty-five acre complex, south of Garfield Park, had many buildings, the most iconic being the original fourteen story "Sears Tower," still standing today. The grounds included a classic garden with pergolas and lushly planted flower beds.

After Jens Jensen rose to the position of general superintendent and chief landscape architect in 1905, he began creating Prairie-style landscapes throughout the parks and boulevards of the West Side. Native plants, water, and stonework were important aspects of Jensen's evolving design ideas. In Humboldt Park, he extended the existing lagoon into a long meandering waterway that was evocative of natural scenery he had observed in Illinois and Wisconsin.

In 1918, Jensen designed his masterpiece, Columbus Park. Located west of Garfield Park and bordering Oak Park, Columbus was the largest entirely new park that Jensen designed in Chicago. Each of its elements, including an expansive prairie river with stratified stone waterfalls, expressed his style and philosophies. According to Jensen, these features symbolized "a bit of native Illinois along our rivers so to give the city dweller and especially youth something of his native land that he otherwise would never see."[4]

PURSUING THE AMERICAN DREAM

Chicago's Maxwell Street neighborhood had long provided a port of entry for European immigrants who came in pursuit of the American Dream. Despite their expectations, life was often very difficult. In response, Jane Addams opened one of the nation's first settlement houses at 800 South Halsted Street. Hull House provided social, educational, and cultural services to diverse groups of people in need.

Many immigrants moved westward into the neighborhoods bordering Garfield Park as industry grew in surrounding areas and new jobs became available. The three major employers were Sears, Roebuck and Company, McCormick Reaper Works (later known as International Harvester), and the Western Electric plant, which was located in suburban Cicero.

By the early 1900s, new immigrants joined the existing populations of Irish, German, Polish, and Scandinavian descent. Within this area mostly composed of white residents, an

African American neighborhood also flourished. This small black community was located near West Lake Street and North Western Avenue between Union and Garfield parks.

During World War I, European immigration slowed while the number of manufacturing jobs in Chicago increased. This opened new opportunities for African Americans, who had previously been excluded from such factory work. Tens of thousands of black people moved from the rural South to Chicago during the Great Migration. Like European immigrants, they were also pursuing the American Dream. Between 1900 and 1920, the city's African American population grew from 30,000 to more than 100,000. While most of the new black residents settled on Chicago's South Side, others joined the West Side enclave.

Some of the West Side's African Americans worked as laborers and maids while others established businesses on West Warren Boulevard and West Lake Street under the elevated structure. There were black-owned bakeries, restaurants, laundries, butcher shops, funeral homes, and clothing stores. Edward Johnson's family owned the Lake Street Hatters which made new hats and mended old ones. College-educated black professionals lived and worked in the community as teachers, lawyers, and doctors. Many of them, such as Dr. Fred Jesse Braxton, who was a dentist, had clients of both races.[5]

The neighborhood had modest homes on attractive tree-lined streets. One early resident recalled, "Vegetables were grown in the back yard and flowers, including tall sunflowers grew in the small front yard. We raised chickens and fattened ducks and turkeys for the holidays."[6] Some blocks were racially integrated, and residents later reminisced that "everybody's children were in each other's house…and it didn't make any difference."[7]

AN "ADJUSTED NEIGHBORHOOD"

By 1919, the neighborhood between Garfield and Union parks was approximately sixty percent white and forty percent black, one of the city's most racially balanced. Although a terrible week-long race riot broke out on the South Side that year, the West Side enclave remained harmonious. As a result of the violence that had been pervasive throughout much of Chicago, Governor Lowden formed a commission to study and improve race relations. In its report, *The Negro in Chicago*, the commission described this part of the city as an "adjusted neighborhood," because it was racially integrated.[8]

The study also included data about the limited public services and facilities available to Chicago's black population. It described Union Park as one of the few parks in the city that offered full access to African Americans. The report explained that when the West Park

Commissioners built a natatorium, reading room, and playground, they distributed flyers inviting the black community to enjoy the new facilities along with the white park patrons.[9]

By the late 1920s, Union Park had a staff of talented black professionals who taught classes and organized activities. Mrs. Anna Walker—born, raised, and college-educated in North Carolina—began working as the park's drama and music instructor in 1926. She was among the earliest black women to serve in a professional position for the West Park Commission.

Left: Mrs. Anna Walker and the Union Park Orchestra, 1935. During the Depression years, Union Park was the cultural center of the West Side's African American community. Right: Union Park swimming pool, ca. 1920.

MELTING POT

In the 1920s, while larger numbers of Jewish and Italian families were moving in, the neighborhoods near Garfield Park still retained the character of some of the earlier populations. The older Irish community continued to celebrate its cultural identity. It held an annual St. Patrick's Day Parade, which began at the bandstand in Garfield Park and attracted 100,000 spectators. The Garfield Park Conservatory often had a special display of real shamrocks in observance of the holiday.

While the neighborhood had dozens of Catholic and Protestant churches, it also had a large concentration of Jewish residents. Chicago's Jewish population now totaled 300,000, making it the third largest of any city in the world, following only New York City and Warsaw, Poland. Vast numbers of Russian Jews had moved into North Lawndale after World War I.

Left: Man blowing shofar for the Jewish holiday, Rosh Hashanah, ca. 1930. Right: Banquet at Jewish Home for the Aged at 16th Street and Albany Avenue, ca. 1930. Today, alumni of nearby Marshall High School recall that the school emptied out during the Jewish holidays.

By 1930, Jewish people made up fifty percent of the neighborhood population. "Chicago's Jerusalem" became a hub for synagogues, schools, and related organizations.[10] Because of its density, the Jewish community spilled over into the East and West Garfield Park neighborhoods just to the north.

The B'nai B'rith Youth Organization and other Jewish groups sponsored tournaments and cultural activities that took place in the parks and along the boulevards. Garfield Park's band stand served as the locus for a festival to celebrate the ancient Jewish festival of Shavuot in the 1930s. During the High Holy Days, thousands of people gathered at Douglas Park's lagoon to symbolically cast their sins into the water, as part of a Jewish tradition known as *Tashlich*. Many organizations held Channukah celebrations, Mahjong parties, dances, lectures, and meetings at the Midwest Athletic Club, a stately fourteen-story building at the corner of North Hamlin Avenue and West Madison Street. The Graemere, an elegant residential hotel east of Garfield Park, hosted similar events.

The Italian community was extremely active during this period, often utilizing the same facilities. The Italian-American Civic League held a convention at the Midwest Athletic Club, attracting 1500 participants from all over the country. In 1934, Italian Consul General Giuseppe Castruccio spoke to the West Side Kiwanis Club.[11] Along with many other organizations, the Italian Chamber of Commerce, Italian World War Veterans, and the Sons of Italy held social and civic events in the Garfield Park area.

DEPRESSION ERA

Like so many other Americans, Chicagoans suffered from the difficulties of the Great Depression in the 1930s. At the time, *The Nation* reported:

> "Chicago is in desperate need. It cannot pay its debts; it cannot feed its hungry. Here there are 700,000 men and women without work, more than 100,000 families on the dole."[12]

Feelings of hopefulness were ignited when Franklin Delano Roosevelt won the presidential nomination at the 1932 Democratic Convention in the Chicago Stadium, then located at 1800 West Madison Street. Roosevelt's acceptance speech was played on the radio while many West Siders heard it broadcast from speakers that were hung in the trees in nearby Union Park.

After his election, President Roosevelt created the Works Progress Administration (WPA) to stimulate economic recovery. The newly consolidated Chicago Park District used WPA funds to make improvements to the parks and boulevards and provide recreational and cultural programs. Through the WPA, the Chicago Recreation Commission also opened twenty-nine West Side community centers.

Despite government funding, many people were still in dire need. Community and religious groups organized parties and special events that not only brightened their dreary days, but helped West Siders directly. Churches held bingo and Bunco nights as fundraisers. Among the efforts sponsored by Jewish charities was a city summer camp for West Side

Left: Unemployed squatters on the West Side, 1932.
Right: Men carrying sandwich signs during the Great Depression, 1934.

"My mother and father brought much of the way of their living in Louisiana to Chicago. In the front yard she had flowers. In the back yard she grew carrots and onions and tomatoes. Just grew them to eat."

— Reverend Eudora Ramey

"We observed African American people looking for apartments, and generally speaking, when African American people first moved in…everything was upgraded because they were putting in their gardens — much more nature-oriented."

— Beverly Chubat

Connie family home at 2302 West Fulton Street, ca. 1940.

boys who could not "afford to attend a country camp."[13] Businesses tried to do their part by pledging to create jobs and hosting fundraising benefits.

Throughout the West Side, the land itself provided a valuable resource. The Joint Emergency Relief commission coordinated efforts to offer garden plots to the needy. The commission prepared the ground and furnished free seeds. At least 1,800 plots were allotted throughout the neighborhood for unemployed people to plant, tend, and harvest, thereby providing food for the hungry.

GOOD TIMES DURING HARD TIMES

West Side festivals and parades tempered the hardships of the 1930s and engendered ethnic pride. The Chicago *Golden Gloves* elite amateur boxing championships, which were held annually at the Chicago Stadium, sparked many neighborhood celebrations. When boxers came to America from various European countries, locals of the same heritage held elaborate receptions for them here. The Italians were especially enthusiastic, organizing lively welcoming parades with dozens of bands, often culminating in large festivals in Garfield Park.

In 1935, event organizer Arch Ward wrote:

> "Many nationalities other than Italian will be represented in the crowd, for the celebration is for everybody— Germans, Jews, Irish, Poles, French, Scandinavians. All who make up the great west side population are welcome at this festival, which is designed to show the visitors from Italy how hospitable and sportsmanlike Chicago can be."[14]

Left: Audience at the *West Chicagoland Music Festival*, ca. 1940. Right: *Golden Gloves* boxers in the 135 pound category, 1936. The Golden Gloves tournament featured many boxers from the Catholic Youth Organization's team including Andy Scrivani, a West Side Italian, and James Martin, an African American who had moved to Chicago from Mississippi.

135 POUND DIVISION

No. 1—ANDY SCRIVANI, a member of the C. Y. O. team, was the Golden Gloves 126 pound champion last year. He has held C. Y. O. titles in the 118, 126 and 135 pound divisions. He is an Italian lad from Chicago's west side and is rated by many as one of the best amateur boxers ever developed in Chicago. He has been boxing for three years and is 18 years of age.

No. 2—JAMES MARTIN is another C. Y. O. representative. He is 20 years old and is a high school student. He won the Golden Gloves novice lightweight championship last year, less than six months after he had started boxing. He was born in Greenville, Miss., but came to Chicago when a youngster. When able to get a job, he works as a laborer.

Another annual celebration that attracted huge and diverse audiences to the area, the *West Chicagoland Musical Festival* was presented and performed by African Americans and attended by "community residents of all colors."[15] Anna Walker, who directed Union Park's cultural activities, organized the event with help from a volunteer Women's Auxilary. They spent months raising money, soliciting sponsorships from surrounding businesses, and planning the festivities.

Each year, a parade circled west of Union Park to mark the beginning of the two-day festival. "Negro bands and boy scout troops, Sunday school softball teams and festival queens with their ladies in waiting" all participated in the parade.[16] The evenings were filled with music, drama, dance, and other entertainment. Walker was able to attract prominent musicians such as Keen Fleming's Orchestra and the father of gospel, Thomas A. Dorsey, with his 500-voice choir. This vibrant annual festival continued after the Depression through the 1940s.

THE HOMEFRONT

During World War II, West Siders pulled together to help with the nation's efforts at home. As men were shipped off to the fighting fronts, women helped out in various ways. They were involved in civil defense activities and many filled in for men by taking jobs in West Side defense plants. Women employed by the Cinch Manufacturing Corporation on West Van Buren Street made parts for gas masks, jeeps, and military communications equipment.

While white women found new employment opportunities, African Americans of both genders had difficulties. In cooperation with other groups, the Urban League of Chicago's West Side office campaigned "for more Negroes as skilled laborers in defense plants."[17]

Patriotism and civic pride inspired West Siders to improve their own communities by transforming vacant lots into Victory Gardens. Because food and other rations were scarce, a "…civilian army equipped with rakes and hoes" planted empty lots which soon "…burst forth into neat rows of cabbages, tomatoes, and lettuce."[18]

The Garfield Park Businessmen's Association (formerly the Garfield Park Club) had organized annual clean-up drives for years. These "Clean Up, Paint Up, Light Up," campaigns involving thousands of local scouts and school children thrived during the 1940s.[19] The "flower garden girls" from Lucy Flower Technical School carried signs to encourage people to clean and plant their backyards.[20] Mops, dust pans, paint, and paint brushes were passed out in this orchestrated spring cleaning effort. "A window box in every home and a garbage can in every back yard" were encouraged.[21]

MADISON-CRAWFORD COMEBACK

The Garfield Park Businessmen's Association focused primarily on the Madison-Crawford shopping district, an area that flourished in the Jazz Age with elegant clubs, restaurants, and theatres, but struggled through the Depression. After World War II, old stores received facelifts and new ones sprang up. Goldblatt's department store opened in 1951, providing a retail anchor in the business district. Then heralded as one of the city's most modern commercial buildings, the store had an open floor plan with central air conditioning. The other large department stores were Madigan Brothers and Baer Brothers & Prodie which celebrated its fiftieth anniversary in 1951.

The bustling district had many different kinds of shops, bakeries, banks, lounges, and restaurants such as Little Jack's. Fanciful movie palaces like the four-thousand-seat Marbro and the Art Moderne-style Alex (previously the Hamlin Theater) flourished. Mom and pop establishments had their own personalities. For example, Barney Fornero, "the singing barber," serenaded his customers while cutting their hair.[22]

The Garfield Park Businessmen's Association vehemently fought the renaming of Crawford Avenue as Pulaski Road. This proposal honoring Casimir Pulaski was sponsored by the Democratic machine to please the city's large Polish population. After nearly twenty-two years, the business association lost its legal battle, and the street became Pulaski Road in 1952.

Left: Alex Theatre at 3826 West Madison Street, 1972.
Right: People entering Goldblatt's on West Madison Street, ca. 1955.

"Madison Street was a very good shopping area. It had very nice theatres…The Marbro and the Paradise which had clouds and stars on the ceiling. We used to go to Roosevelt Road and we'd go to Flukeys and the hot dogs were five cents and the waitresses carried them on their arm, five or six hot dogs on an arm."

— Bernard Sahlins

"The shopping was good! You had stores called Madigans, Three Sisters, Goldblatt's. We would go shopping, and they had a theater in the neighborhood called the Marbro. That was cool…but it was torn down."

— Mattie Simpson

View of West Madison Street looking east from Pulaski Road, ca. 1955.

WEAR AND TEAR

Despite the thriving business district, by the 1950s, the West Side was showing signs of wear. Much of its older housing stock had become severely deteriorated. For decades, single-family homes and two-flats had been converted into many smaller units to accommodate a growing population.

A second wave of African Americans from the South migrated to Chicago seeking better job opportunities. For years, restrictive housing covenants had effectively barred African Americans from living in the neighborhoods of their choice. A 1948 United States Supreme Court decision lifted those covenants, opening the door to previously prohibited areas. Residents of the dense South Side "Black Belt" moved to the West Side in hopes of finding more space and better housing. Although this area proved to be fairly crowded, it had a warm and welcoming atmosphere. Newcomers who settled here from the rural south and Chicago's South Side often declared "the West Side is the best side." [23]

Their enthusiasm often persisted despite difficult living conditions. Much of the area was overrun with substandard apartments neglected by absentee landlords. Many of those who had purchased their own homes had trouble securing home improvement loans because of prejudicial bank practices.

In the early 1950s, the West Side was in the path of a proposed super highway. The Congress Expressway, now known as the Eisenhower, not only provided for automobile traffic but also included a rapid transit line in the center median. Although West Siders

Left: Corner of South Kedzie Avenue and West Congress Street, 1946. Blocks of brick and masonry structures were sacrificed to make way for the Congress Expressway. Right: Congress Expressway with Rapid Transit line in the center, 1960. This is now I 290, the Eisenhower Expressway.

initially believed that the super highway would bring additional trade to the area, ultimately it had the opposite effect. Hundreds of homes, businesses, and industrial plants were torn down, permanently displacing thousands of people. The Congress Expressway actually made the suburbs a more convenient place for commerce. Major West Side businesses began leaving the city as the highway was finished in the late 1950s.

In hopes of boosting the area's economy, many community members rallied behind a plan to build a Chicago campus for the University of Illinois in Garfield Park. University administrators focused on three possible locations, with the 135-acre site in Garfield Park as their first choice. Despite the potential loss of valuable green space, there was strong community support for the proposal. The Chicago Motor Club voiced some opposition, warning that this plan would wreak havoc on West Side traffic. Architectural historian Carl Condit called the concept of sacrificing parkland for the university campus an "…act of vandalism comparable to killing zoo animals or mutilating the paintings in the Art Institute."[24] A committee of more than a dozen civic groups and local businesses formed to fight the proposal. Mayor Richard J. Daley preferred the site southwest of downtown. In 1962, Mayor Daley's plan prevailed, and the new campus in Little Italy opened three years later.

CHANGING TIMES

By the early 1960s, much of the West Side was racially mixed. Older West Siders alive today recall a time when black and white neighbors lived alongside each other harmoniously.

Better Boys Foundation board meeting, ca. 1965.

Teenagers attended Marshall High School together and adults cooperated on efforts such as cleaning the neighborhood and sweeping out the alleys.

Hopes for sustaining a racially integrated West Side, however, were hindered by the manipulative practice of "blockbusting." Unscrupulous real estate agents and speculators would purchase a house on an all-white block and move in the first black family. Using a variety of tactics, they pressured adjacent owners into selling at rates far below market value. They would then resell to African American families at extremely inflated prices.

According to historian Amanda Seligman, many West Siders abhorred blockbusters. She cites the *Garfieldian*, a neighborhood newspaper, which "freely referred to speculators as 'sharks'."[25] In her book *Block by Block*, Seligman reprinted an editorial cartoon of a monster depicted as a:

> "...'Real Estate Speculator' stomping on communities of single family homes. In addition to the warning 'Beware This,' the cartoonist offered 'apologies to Dracula, Werewolf, and Frankenstein' for slandering them by associating them with blockbusters."[26]

These "panic peddlers" contributed to a mass exodus of white residents from the West Side.

Reverend James Stone leading Dr. Martin Luther King, Jr. to pulpit, ca. 1965. This event was held in the Stone Temple Baptist Church on West Douglas Boulevard.

STRIVING FOR BETTER CONDITIONS

Overcrowding and poor housing conditions were not the only problems faced by West Siders in the mid-1960s. They were dealing with high rates of unemployment, poverty, and crime. These mounting problems prompted the formation of groups to help the needy and address broad neighborhood issues. The Daughters of Charity established the Marillac House, a Catholic social center just east of Garfield Park. The Midwest Community Council focused on better housing, new schools, improved community facilities, better law enforcement, and jobs. The Chicago Urban League's West Side office also sought increased employment opportunities, which would "certainly reduce juvenile delinquency and crime rates in the area."[27]

The realities of the inner city often overwhelmed good intentions. Vacant, dilapidated, and boarded-up buildings were becoming hang-outs for neighborhood teens, contributing to crime and delinquency. The need for housing reform in cities throughout America was a major focus of the civil rights movement. To bring national attention to the plight of disadvantaged African Americans and the conditions in which they lived, Dr. Martin Luther

King, Jr. moved his young family from Atlanta into an apartment in North Lawndale in 1966. In this historic "drive against slum conditions," Dr. King urged West Siders to pressure for improvements in housing, employment, and education.[28]

RIOTS AND AFTERMATH

On April 5, 1968, the day after the assassination of Dr. Martin Luther King, Jr., rioting erupted in inner-city neighborhoods throughout the nation. Years of frustration on Chicago's West Side exploded into destructive mob violence. Dozens of buildings were set on fire, particularly along West Madison Street. After rioters began attacking police and firefighters with rocks, bricks, and knives, Mayor Daley called in the National Guard, which did not arrive for many hours.

Residents in the twelve-square-mile riot zone were also under attack. Many stayed up all night guarding their homes and businesses. Despite such efforts, the riots destroyed 175 buildings and drove hundreds of families from their homes. After three days of havoc, seven people had died, five hundred were injured, and nearly three thousand were arrested.

Although the angry mobs had gathered at the edge of Garfield Park and rioted in the adjacent streets, the park itself was left untouched. John A. Lundgren, Chief Horticulturalist expressed his surprise when he returned to work after the riots and "…only found one broken soda bottle on the walk and no damage to grass or flowers."[29]

Left: View of Garfield Park Conservatory looking north from under West Lake Street "L," 1968.
Right: West Madison Street shortly after riots, 1968.

Newspapers reported that after the devastation, the area's residents "…wound up worse off than ever—with fewer stores and homes, with buildings still more dilapidated."[30] Many middle-class black families decided to move farther west into the Austin community or to Chicago's suburbs. Owners of stores and businesses often had no choice but to leave when insurance companies raised premiums or cancelled their policies altogether. International Harvester, one of the area's largest employers, pulled out in 1969, taking away 3,400 jobs. The other major employer, Sears, Roebuck & Co., closed most of its West Side operation in the early 1970s, when it built the new Sears Tower, a downtown skyscraper. Nevertheless, numerous residents continued to live on the West Side and remained committed to improving the area despite its mounting problems.

A STRUGGLE FOR SERVICES

Of all of the issues with which the West Side contended, housing had reached a crisis level. Even though the riots contributed to a dwindling population, the available housing stock remained terribly inadequate. "During one period between January 1970 and June 1973, only 91 new units were built while 2,714 were demolished."[31] The Chicago Housing Authority had built several complexes at mid-century, but by the 1980s, conditions in them had become deplorable. Other available residential buildings continued to deteriorate. Over the next couple of decades the City began razing thousands of dangerously substandard structures, resulting in 1,750 vacant lots in East Garfield Park alone.[32]

Housing issues were compounded by unemployment, poverty and a rising crime rate. In the face of such dire problems, City services fell grievously short. Community organizations struggled to make the government agencies face the area's looming problems:

"Things you take for granted in other parts of the city have to be struggled for here, over and over again…Good schools, housing, jobs, recreational facilities, police courtesy. We're still battling lead poisoning! Even having the garbage picked up by the city is a struggle." [33]

Nancy Jefferson, executive director of the Midwest Community Council expressed these frustrations in 1980. Jefferson worked diligently with hundreds of churches and block clubs. Other groups such as the East Garfield Park Community Union, Bethel New Life, and Lawndale's Pyramidwest Development Corporation were equally committed to revitalizing the community. These civic organizations found greater success after the 1983 election of Mayor Harold Washington who was especially concerned about Chicago's neighborhoods and all of the racial and ethnic groups within them.

VISIBLE SIGNS OF REINVESTMENT

After the Sears Headquarters sat largely vacant for years, in the late 1980s, developer Charles H. Shaw envisioned its transformation as a catalyst for reinvigorating the community. With support of the City of Chicago, Chicago Park District, and dedicated citizens, Shaw created Homan Square, an innovative redevelopment project that provided mixed-income housing and attracted the middle-class back to the area.

Other visible signs of reinvestment surfaced on Chicago's West Side in the 1990s. The United Center, one of the nation's largest sports arenas, replaced the old Chicago Stadium

Left: Homan Square, 2007. Right: Garden at Homan Square, 2007.

"We blacks lived like a family. The adults were always visible and you know you couldn't leave the house and act up here because everybody knew everybody…Everybody knew who's little girl or boy you were. And if they saw you doing something you weren't supposed to do, they'd chastise you and your parents."

—Reverend Eudora Ramey

"The neighborhood surrounding the Garfield Park really means a lot to me…Even when we decided to move we only moved right across the street. This is where my friends are and where I feel welcomed and comfortable. Everyone around here that I know is like family."

—Yolandis M., Green Teen, age 14

Family in Garfield Park, 2007.

in 1994. To prompt development in East Garfield Park, the area was designated as a Federal Empowerment Zone, and began receiving state funds through Illinois FIRST (Fund for Infrastructure, Roads, Schools, and Transit) to eliminate drugs and develop vacant lots in the community.

The Garfield Park Conservatory's nearest "L" station at West Homan Avenue closed in 1992. As part of a $300 million rehabilitation of the Green Line "L" that began in 1999, the Chicago Transit Authority relocated the station even closer to the conservatory at North Central Park Avenue and West Lake Street. The CTA moved elements of the old North Homan Avenue station and used them to reconstruct the station at its new location.

COMMUNITY GARDENS FLOURISH

For many years, community gardening has been a vehicle to stabilize and beautify the West Side. North Lawndale residents Gerald and Lorean Earles formed "Slum Busters" in 1986. Since then, the organization has been planting lush flower and vegetable gardens in vacant lots throughout the neighborhood. The Chicago Urban Gardening Program has helped other civic groups transform fallow spaces into productive gardens.

By the early twenty-first century, approximately one hundred community gardens were flourishing on the West Side. Clarence McAlpin, a local volunteer decided to plant an African heritage garden on South Central Park Avenue and West 12th Place. He said: "It would look kind of funny to have a Chinese or Japanese garden because everyone here is of African descent."[34] After researching plants that could be found in Africa, he and other residents planted impatiens, geraniums, peanuts, aloe vera, watermelon, kale, and a flower bed shaped like the continent of Africa.[35]

CONSERVATORY AS COMMUNITY ASSET

The formation of the Garfield Park Conservatory Alliance has spurred an unprecedented partnership among West Side residents, community and greening organizations, and the Chicago Park District. The partnership has established the conservatory as an important community asset.

The conservatory serves the community in a variety of ways. In 2002, during the Garfield Park Framework Planning Process, local residents suggested using part of the maintenance yards north of the conservatory as a stimulus for the local economy. The old horse sheds

Conservatory-Central Park Green Line "L" station, 2007.

Left: Bethel New Life Commercial Center, 2007. This mixed-use facility relies on the newest "green" technologies. Right: Garfield Park Market Place, 2005. The Market Place represents the first phase of converting old maintenance areas of Garfield Park into public spaces.

and adjacent alley were converted into the Garfield Market Place. In this venue, visitors can purchase plants, produce, unique garden elements, artworks, and often see artists at work. In 2003, a group of Moroccan craftsmen created a beautiful fountain of mosaic tile in one of the Garfield Market Place sheds. Sponsored by the Sister Cities Program, the fountain, named *Zellij* was later installed in Horticulture Hall.

Because of its impact in the community, the Garfield Park Conservatory Alliance was chosen by the Local Initiatives Support Corporation (LISC) to lead their New Communities Program. LISC supports inner-city neighborhoods throughout the nation and is devoted to improving several West Side communities such as West Haven, North Lawndale, and East Garfield Park.

The Alliance provides valuable programs to the community such as early childhood literacy initiatives and an after-school program called the Flower House Kids. The Green Teens is an environmentally-based program for West Side high school students emphasizing job skills and mentoring relationships between students and business professionals. Partnerships with local organizations have resulted in the investment of more one million dollars in the community. These include a job-training program for ex-offenders and an educational and cultural exchange between neighborhood high school students and young people from Ghana.

The Alliance's New Communities Program has also worked with hundreds of East Garfield Park stakeholders to produce a Quality of Life Plan for the neighborhood. The plan has developed strategies such as reusing vacant lots, managing growth and gentrification, and using greening as a vehicle for positive change. This initiative has led to a Neighborhood

Development Council which has become active in promoting retail growth, staging cultural events, facilitating greening projects, and raising awareness of health issues.

GREEN REVOLUTION

The Garfield Park Conservatory's community initiatives have helped spark a "green revolution" throughout the West Side. Openlands (previously called the Openlands Project) and the East Garfield Park Neighborhood Development Council produced an Open Space Plan recommending lush gardens, more public green spaces, improved streetscapes, and environmentally sound businesses. Just east of the conservatory, the City of Chicago transformed a "brownfield" site into the Center for Green Technology. Since opening to the public in 2002, the center has been providing homeowners and businesses with information about innovative and cost-efficient environmental practices. This resource serves as a hub for the area's new "green business" district. Bethel New Life is using energy efficient technologies for affordable housing developments. It also has built the Bethel Commercial Center, a mixed-use transit center with retail, employment training, and day-care facilities. Located west of Garfield Park, the environmentally sustainable building has solar panels and a green roof.

In 2005, vacant ground on the old Sears Roebuck and Company site became a unique combination of community gardens and beehives operated by the Chicago Honey Co-op. Some of the land has reverted to pre-settlement prairie flowers such as goldenrod and milkweed, good sources of nectar for the bees to collect. The beekeeping cooperative provides jobs to area residents who tend one hundred hives and help produce chemical-free honey and related products.

LIVING LANDMARK

At the Garfield Park Conservatory's 100th birthday in 2008, West Siders have much to celebrate. The conservatory is a living landmark that breathes new life into its surrounding community. The beneficial aspects of nature can be felt throughout the West Side. The ideology of the conservatory's designer Jens Jensen resonates today:

> "To come in contact with living plants is an inspiration to the mind that brings the body well-being and content. It is a new world for the city-bred that broadens out his vision and makes him better fitted for the struggle of existence."[36] ❖

Top: Chicago Center for Green Technology, 2007. Located at 445 North Sacramento Boulevard, the center is operated by the Chicago Department of Environment. Bottom: Beekeepers at the Chicago Honey Co-op, 2007.

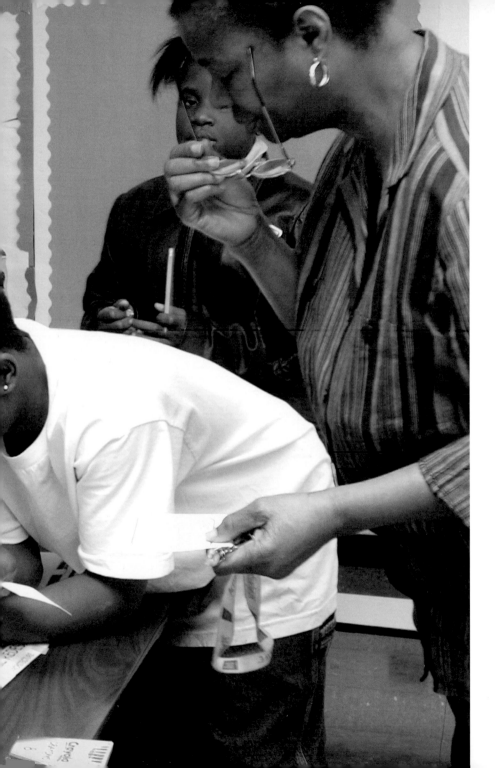

"My neighborhood is special to me because this is where all of my memories are. I consider this place my home. My neighborhood has helped me grow into the young woman I am today."

—Laqueda W., Green Teen, age 15

"This week I went past Garfield Park and saw some people shoveling the snow and they were all working together. I can't wait for the summer to see the nature looking beautiful."

—Ashley S., Willa Cather Elementary School

"It was just a glorious place to live, the proximity to the city and the openness and the wonderful neighborhood feeling."

—Diane Kelley

Landscape architecture students from the University of Illinois (Champaign-Urbana) at a planning workshop with students from Willa Cather Elementary School, 2007.

"When I came in the neighborhood it was before the riots, so everything was busy on Madison…Two civil rights scouts would come to my place at Madison and Albany. Bennett and Ann, they'd sit there and they didn't order much. They asked would I like to have some more customers. I said to myself 'How are they going to bring me more customers?' But I said, 'Sure, I'd love more customers.' Dorothy Tilman, Jesse Jackson, and all these civil rights workers started coming. One day, Dr. King came in. Don't ask what he ate."

—Edna Stewart, Proprietor of Edna's Restaurant

Edna Stewart, 2007. Edna's famous soul food restaurant is located at 3175 West Madison Street.

Niki Nights event sponsored by the Garfield
Park Conservatory Alliance, 2007.

················· ABOUT THE ALLIANCE ·················

The independent, not-for-profit Garfield Park Conservatory Alliance was incorporated in 1998 to support the revitalization of the Garfield Park Conservatory and to
ensure that local West Side neighborhoods would benefit from this revitalization.
Since its inception, efforts have focused on utilizing the conservatory's renowned
collections to increase visitors' knowledge about plants and the environment. The Alliance
presents educational programs for children, teachers, and gardeners, collaborates with the
Chicago Park District in managing major exhibitions including *Chihuly in the Park* (2001–
02) and *Niki in the Garden* (2007), and through a partnership with Local Initiatives Support
Corporation, serves as the lead agency for the East Garfield Park New Communities
Program. The Garfield Park Conservatory Alliance builds community through the unique
combination of people, plants, and place.

The Alliance has published this book in honor of the Centennial of the Garfield Park
Conservatory, and is thankful for support from:

> *Chicago Park District*
> *Sara Lee Foundation, Lead Corporate Sponsor*
> *Chicago Public Schools*
> *The Richard H. Driehaus Foundation*

The Alliance is also grateful to the Parkways Foundation for commissioning Alex Kotlowitz
to write the foreword for *Inspired by Nature: The Garfield Park Conservatory and Chicago's West
Side*. This was made possible by the following donors: Julia S. Bachrach, Karen Goodyear,
Donna LaPietra, Jackie McKay, Cindy Mitchell, Stuart Nathan, Brenda Palm, Myra Reilly,
and Diane Sprenger.

Epilogue

by Eunita Rushing

History usually repeats itself, but at the Garfield Park Conservatory, history *surges forward*. We celebrate the legacy of Jens Jensen by re-engaging and by re-igniting a passion for the beauty, life, and green on the West Side of Chicago. One hundred long years have been compressed into the last ten, moving us closer to the unity of plants and people envisioned by Jensen. This renewed commitment catapults the conservatory and the Garfield Park community into our second century—the era we have all anticipated.

Our expectations continually leap forward. Like a vibrant scent emanating from a flower, our memories and personal experiences at the conservatory bring us back, first to the past, then back to the forefront. This bond is not just in the facility. The community, like the conservatory, was never lost unto itself. Those outside the community are rediscovering the West Side as it continues to subsist, sustain, reposition, and soar.

Partnerships between organizations, including the strong collaboration between the Chicago Park District and the Garfield Park Conservatory Alliance, offer limitless possibilities. For the past decade, the Alliance has supported the revitalization of the Garfield Park Conservatory and ensured that local West Side neighborhoods benefit from the revitalization. Since its inception, the Alliance has focused on utilizing the conservatory's renowned collections to increase visitors' knowledge about plants and the environment. The Alliance presents educational programs for children, teachers, and gardeners, and collaborates with the Chicago Park District on major exhibitions and special events. We honor the legacy of Jens Jensen and continue to build and grow strong—deeply inspired by nature—as the city, country, and the conservatory use greening and plants as a backdrop for securing and building the next hundred years.

The people have reclaimed the conservatory—the jewel of the West Side. They own it and acknowledge it as a part of the community's foundation, both today and tomorrow. By striving for excellence and growing programs that speak to the heart of the people, the Garfield Park Conservatory Alliance has created a new energy. This energy engulfs and transports many: those who embrace history, life, and the future; those who embrace nature; those who educate and inspire; those who study science and botany; and the social activists who cry for justice. All converge at the cultural hub—the conservatory—to build a sustained momentum for a people, a community for another century of progress.

Eunita Rushing is President of the Garfield Park Conservatory Alliance.

141

The West side has a rich history that has shaped the very essence of today's parks, boulevards, and communities from the early years, beginning with the West Park Commission, to today, with the Chicago Park District. I share in the pride of this neighborhood and its early leaders who laid the foundation for three of our most prominent parks—Douglas, Garfield, and Humboldt—providing nature in the midst of a concrete jungle. At the center is one of the largest, most impressive conservatories in the country—the Garfield Park Conservatory. Connecting nature to arts and culture, the conservatory is regarded by many as Chicago's premier cultural and botanic institution.

Partnerships have helped resurrect and revitalize the West Side. Since 1998, the Chicago Park District and the Garfield Park Conservatory Alliance have worked together to strengthen the community, offering visitors opportunities to make connections between plants and their own lives. This vital partnership has also helped the conservatory reach out to the community. The innovative programs provided by our partner, along with the preservation and maintenance of a magnificent cultural facility, enhances the environmental, social, and economic vitality of Chicago's West Side. We encourage more community involvement to attract not only local visitors, but national and international tourists as well.

The Chicago Park District will continue this mission by focusing on four core values: accessibility, fitness, environmental stewardship, and partnerships. Priorities include: the City Garden Phase II at the Garfield Park Conservatory; a new playground in Garfield Park, which opened in June 2007; the rehabilitation of the prominent and historic Gold Dome in Garfield Park; the rehabilitation of the Sweet House into a new exhibit called *Sugar From the Sun* at the Conservatory opening in 2008; new playground construction in June 2008 in Humboldt Park; the Puerto Rican Arts Center at the Humboldt Park Refectory opening in Fall 2007; and a West Side family aquatics center in Douglas Park, which is the proposed site for a 2016 Olympic Games Aquatics Venue.

The Park District seeks to strengthen this neighborhood's future in cooperation with the Parkways Foundation, the Garfield Park Conservatory Alliance, corporate partners, advisory councils, public officials, and private citizens and organizations. We will enhance quality of life by providing excellent recreation opportunities, beautifully maintained facilities and landscapes, and a customer focused and responsive park system. Our Chicago parks should leave visitors with a memorable experience that will last a lifetime.

Timothy J. Mitchell is General Superintendent & CEO of the Chicago Park District.

1 "Public Parks— A Suggestion," *Chicago Press and Tribune*, August 10, 1858, 0_1.

2 Carter Harrison, "Memoirs," in Caroline Kirkland, ed., *Chicago Yesterdays, A Sheaf of Reminiscences* (Chicago: Daughaday and Company, 1919), 177.

3 Theodore Dreiser, *Sister Carrie* (New York: Doubleday, Page & Co., 1900, reprinted Pennsylvania: University of Pennsylvania Press, 1981), 147.

4 Theodore Turak, *William Le Baron Jenney: A Pioneer of Modern Architecture* (Ann Arbor, Michigan: UMI Research Press, 1986), 78.

5 William Le Baron Jenney, correspondence to Frederick Law Olmsted, September 16, 1865, Olmsted Papers, Library of Congress Manuscript Department.

6 Daniel Bluestone, *Constructing Chicago* (New Haven: Yale University Press, 1991), 26.

7 *Twelfth Annual Report of West Chicago Park Commissioners*, (Chicago: 1881), 8.

8 *Second Annual Report of West Chicago Park Commissioners*, (Chicago, 1871), 66.

9 "Real Estate; An Association of Conveyancers and Real Estate Lawyers. Designs for the South Park— Plans for Improving Central Park on the West Side. The Stock Yards Canal— Real Estate Trade and Transfers for the Week," *Chicago Tribune*, August 7, 1870, 0_3.

10 *Twelfth Annual Report of West Chicago Park Commissioners*, (Chicago: 1881), 8.

11 *Fourth Annual Report of West Chicago Park Commissioners*, (Chicago: 1873), 51.

12 "Central Park: Informal Opening of One of Our New Pleasure Grounds," *Chicago Daily Tribune*, August 30, 1874, 2.

13 *Fifth Annual Report of West Chicago Park Commissioners*, (Chicago: 1874), 51.

14 *Twelfth Annual Report of West Chicago Park Commissioners*, (Chicago: 1881), 27.

15 *Fourteenth Annual Report of West Chicago Park Commissioners*, (Chicago: 1883), 16.

16 *Twenty-Sixth Annual Report of West Chicago Park Commissioners*, (Chicago: 1894), 7.

17 Proceedings of West Chicago Park Commissioners, Dec. 10, 1888, v.2, 774-5.

18 Alfred Caldwell. Personal Interview by Julia Sniderman and Robert E. Grese, January 31, 1987.

19 Jens Jensen, as told to Ragna B. Eskil, "Natural Parks and Gardens," *The Saturday Evening Post*, March 8, 1930, 18.

20 Ibid, 19.

21 *Twenty-Seventh Annual Report of West Chicago Park Commissioners*, (Chicago: 1895), 6-7.

22 "Garfield Park Gymnasium Opens-Five Hundred Turners Participate in Formal Dedication of the Improvement to the Public," *Chicago Daily Tribune*, October 12, 1896, 5.

23 "The Garfield Park Murders," *Chicago Daily Tribune*, September 8, 1892, 4.

24 "He Wants Return for His Taxes; An Irate Property Owner Enjoins the West Park Commissioners—His Complaint," *Chicago Daily Tribune*, April 29, 1890, 3.

25 "Punish Pay Roll Stuffing," *Chicago Daily Tribune*, August 1, 1905, 6.

26 *Thirty-Ninth Annual Report of West Chicago Park Commissioners*, (Chicago: 1907), 36.

27 Jensen as told to Eskil, "Natural Parks and Gardens," 19.

28 Jens Jensen, "Object Lesson in Placing Park Sculpture," *Park and Cemetery*, v. 18, no. 3, May 1908, 320.

29 Jensen as told to Eskil, "Natural Parks and Gardens," 18.

30 Ibid, 19.

31 "Chicago's Park Sculpture Show," Park and Cemetery, v. 19, no. 8, October 1909, 127.

32 *Forty-Seventh Annual Report of West Chicago Park Commissioners*, (Chicago: 1915), 22.

33 "Lowden Charges Against Park Board Listed," *Chicago Daily Tribune*, July 30, 1920, 15.

34 "Ice Boat Races at Franklin Park," *Chicago Daily Tribune*, February 16, 1924, 12.

35 *Fifty-third Annual Report of West Chicago Park Commissioners*, (Chicago: 1922), 18.

36 Julia Sniderman. Bachrach, *The City in a Garden: A Photographic History of Chicago's Parks* (Harrisonburg, VA: Center for American Places, 2001), 24.

37 *Third Annual Report of Chicago Park District*, (Chicago: 1937), 131.

38 Wilfrid Smith, "Silver Skates Officials Set for All Comers," *Chicago Daily Tribune*, December 23, 1936, 22.

39 "WPA Art Exhibit to Open Jan. 10 in Garfield Park," *Chicago Daily Tribune*, January 3, 1937, 8.

40 *Eighth Annual Report of Chicago Park District*, (Chicago: 1942), 17.

41 "Guns to Wipe Out Pillbox in Garfield Park," *Chicago Daily Tribune*, June 17, 1945, W1.

42 "Althea Gibson raps to Kids on Tennis Future," *Chicago Defender*, July 21, 1973, 29.

43 United States of America vs. Chicago Park District, Civil Action No. 827308, filed November 30, 1982.

1 Wilhelm Miller, *The Prairie Spirit in Landscape Gardening*, Circular 184 (Urbana, Illinois: University of Illinois Agricultural Experiment Station, November, 1915), 8.

2 *Second Annual Report of West Chicago Park Commissioners*, (Chicago: 1871), 66.

3 *Seventh Annual Report of West Chicago Park Commissioners*, (Chicago: 1876), 6.

4 "The Far-Western Parks; Features of Humboldt, The Boulevard, And Garfield," *Chicago Daily Tribune*, June 18, 1887, 10.

5 "Finds West Parks a Ruin; President Eckhart Tells Board of Decay and Dilapidation. Little Money for Repair. Greenhouses Are Falling to Pieces and Paving is Worn Out," *Chicago Daily Tribune*, August 9, 1905, 1.

6 Thomas McAdam, "Landscape Gardening Under Glass," *Country Life in America*, v. 21, no. 4, December 15, 1911, 13.

7 Ibid.

8 Liberty Hyde Bailey, *Encyclopedia of Horticulture*, 1914–17, 2669 quoted in August Koch, "The Floral Division of the West Chicago Parks," *Parks & Recreation*, v. XI, no. 2, November–December, 1927, 71.

9 Jens Jensen, as told to Ragna B. Eskil, "Natural Parks and Gardens," The Saturday Evening Post, March 8, 1930, 19.

10 Ibid.

11 Ibid.

12 Ibid.

13 Wilhelm Miller, *The Prairie Spirit in Landscape Gardening*, Circular 184 (Urbana, Illinois: University of Illinois Agricultural Experiment Station, , November, 1915), 8.

14 Board of West Chicago Park Commissioners, *The West Parks and Boulevards of Chicago* (Chicago: August 12, 1913), 9.

15 *Fortieth Annual Report of West Chicago Park Commissioners*, (Chicago: 1908), 48.

16 "Great Park Dome Wood and Putty; West Side Conservatory Tottering Because Inferior Materials Were Used, Say Commissioners," *Chicago Daily Tribune*, Sept. 27, 1909, 1.

17 "Save Park Dome, Board's Aim; Workmen Rush Rebuilding of West Side Conservatory," *Chicago Daily Tribune*, September 28, 1909, 3.

18 *Forty-fifth Annual Report of West Chicago Park Commissioners*, (Chicago: 1913), 114.

19 Ibid.

20 West Chicago Park Commissioners, *Catalog Guide to Garfield Park Conservatory* (Chicago: 1924), 9.

21 *Forty-Ninth Annual Report of the West Chicago Park Commissioners*, (Chicago: 1913), 114.

22 *Fifty-Sixth Annual Report of the West Chicago Park Commissioners*, (Chicago: 1924-25), 41.

23 "Flocking to a Chicago Spectacle; Garfield Park Holds Annual Flower Show," *Chicago Daily Tribune*, April 19, 1931, H7.

24 Ibid.

25 Rita Fitzpartick, "World's Lush Carpet is Laid at city's Feet," *Chicago Daily Tribune*, November 27, 1948, 2.

26 "Leaky-Roof Fairyland," *Chicago Daily Tribune*, March 6, 1948, 12.

27 Julia Sniderman Bachrach "Garfield Park Conservatory," in *AIA Guide to Chicago*, Alice Sinkevitch, ed., Harcourt Inc, 1993, (republished 2004), 310.

28 "Robert Van Tress Retires but Not his Green Thumb," *Chicago Daily Tribune*, November 18, 1967, S_ A4.

29 Joel Cahn, "Fancy, Plain — Plants Steal Show," *Chicago Tribune*, April 10, 1969, W4.

30 Julia Sniderman Bachrach, *The City in a Garden: A Photographic History of Chicago's Parks* (Harrisonburg, VA: Center for American Places, 2001), 28.

31 Ted Knutson, "Weekend Chicago; Spring's budding, so petal on out to the flower sites," *Chicago Tribune*, April 21, 1984, 12.

32 William Mullen, "Plants of Another Time at Risk in Forgotten Garden Garfield Park Conservatory May Cost Millions to Fix," *Chicago Tribune*, January 31, 1994, 1.

33 Jim Ritter, "Fest Draw Chocolate Lovers of All Ages," *Chicago Sun-Times*, February 14, 2000, 27.

34 "Garfield Park Conservatory Alliance Hosts 8th Annual Chocolate Fest," *Chicago Park District Press Release*, January 26, 2007.

35 Kelly Kleiman, "Seeing the Future in Glass," *The Wall Street Journal*, February 15, 2002, W7.

36 Ibid.

37 Nancy Moffett, "Uprooting Mona Lisa of palms is no easy task; But rare double coconut needs to grow even bigger," *Chicago Sun-Times*, February 17, 2003, 20.

38 Ibid.

39 Lee Bey, "A Paradise Under Glass," *Chicago Sun-Times*, June 22, 1998, 12.

The Community

1 "Madison Street Almost Ready for Big Carnival—Arrangement Committee Tells of Plans for Entertainment— Makes Provision for Free Shows." *Chicago Daily Tribune*, August 5, 1903, 15.

2 "Carnival Attractions Draw Thousands To West Madison Street; Parade Opens Carnival—West Madison Street Ablaze with Electric Lights," *Chicago Daily Tribune*, August 13, 1903, 5.

3 Alice Sinkevitch, ed. *AIA Guide to Chicago*, (Orlando: A Harvest Original, Harcourt, Inc. 2004), 363.

4 Jens Jensen. "Swimming Pool and Playground at Columbus Park," *Parks & Recreation Magazine*, v. 11, May–June, 1928, 343.

5 Mrs. Hattie Braxton. Personal interview by Glennon Graham, "Bethel New Life: Looking Backward to Move Forward," Bethel New Life Collection, Chicago Public Library Special Collections and Preservation Division, ca 1989.

6 Marjorie Valentine Garner Love, "My West Side 1934–1974," unpublished manuscript, "Bethel New Life: Looking Backward to Move Forward," Bethel New Life Collection, Chicago Public Library Special Collections and Preservation Division, 1994.

7 Rosa Dandridge. Personal interview by Glennon Graham, "Bethel New Life: Looking Backward to Move Forward," Bethel New Life Collection, Chicago Public Library Special Collections and Preservation Division, ca 1989.

8 Chicago Commission on Race Relations, *The Negro in Chicago: A Study of Race Relations and a Race Riot* (Chicago: University of Chicago Press, 1922), 111.

9 Ibid.

10 Irving Cutler, *The Jews of Chicago: From Shtetl to Suburb* (Urbana: University of Illinois Press, 1996), 211.

11 "Blind Scouts Plan Show of Work Tuesday," *Chicago Daily Tribune*, March 11, 1934, W3.

12 Harold M. Mayer and Richard C. Wade, *Chicago: Growth of a Metropolis* (Chicago: The University of Chicago Press, 1969), 358.

13 "Jewish Charities Open Summer Camp for Boys," *Chicago Daily Tribune*, June 16, 1935, W2.

14 Arch Ward, "Chicago Plans Huge Reception for Italian Boxers; Visitors To Be Welcomed At Garfield Park," *Chicago Daily Tribune*, April 26, 1935, 27.

15 Glennon Graham, "Oasis in the Desert: Union Park and the Development of the Black Community on Chicago's West Side 1930s and 1940s" (presented to The Association for Study of Afro-American Life and History 78th Annual Meeting, October, 1993), 6.

16 "Negroes Hold Annual Music Fete Tomorrow—Parade to Park Will Open Program," *Chicago Daily Tribune, July Daily Tribune*, July 14, 1940, W1.

17 "More War Jobs for Negroes is Group's Project; Young Women Canvas West Side Plants," *Chicago Daily Tribune*, May 3, 1942, W6.

18 "Sandlot Games will Give Way to War Gardens; West Siders Ready for Spring Planting," *Chicago Daily Tribune*, April 26, 1942, W6.

19 School Pupils to Fight Dirt in Annual War; Spring Cleanup is due to Start Tomorrow," *Chicago Daily Tribune*, April 21, 1940, W8.

20 "Parade Spreads Cleanup Campaign on West Side," *Chicago Daily Tribune*, April 26, 1940, 24.

21 "School Pupils to Fight Dirt in Annual War; Spring Cleanup is due to Start Tomorrow," *Chicago Daily Tribune*, April 21, 1940, W8.

22 "Barney the Barber Trims Heat Waves for Colleagues" Garfieldian, West Garfield Park Community Collection, Chicago Public Library Special Collections and Preservation Division, n.d.

23 East Garfield Park Neighborhood Development Council and Openlands, "An Open Space Plan for East Garfield Park," October, 2005, 17, www.openlands.org/reports/EGPOpenSpacePlan.pdf.

24 Carl W. Condit, Mrs. R.L. Bradley, Lawrence Rellis, Clayton T. Krein, "An Act if Vandalism," *Chicago Daily Tribune*, April 7, 1960, 20.

25 Amanda Irene Seligman, "'Apologies to Dracula, Werewolf, Frankenstein': White Homeowners and Blockbusters in Postwar Chicago," Journal of the Illinois State Historical Society, vol. 94, no. 1 (Spring 2001): 82.

26 Amanda I. Seligman, *Block By Block: Neighborhoods and Public Policy on Chicago's West Side* (Chicago: University of Chicago Press, 2005), 160.

27 "The Urban League and A West Side Story," *Chicago Daily Defender*, August 4, 1965, 13.

28 "Dr. King to Rent Slum Apartment—Negro Leader to Head Drive from Flat in Chicago," *New York Times*, Jan 21, 1966 51.

29 Jeannye Thornton, "Garfield Park Haven: Conservatory Survives Crisis," *Chicago Tribune*, November 5, 1972, N4.

30 "The Riot; The Place Riot 'King was only the immediate catalyst that catalyst a lifetime of frustration and inhibition'," *Chicago Tribune*, July 28, 1968, J34.

31 Chicago Fact Book Consortium, *Local Community Fact Book, Chicago Metropolitan Area: Based on the 1970 and 1980 Censuses.* (Chicago: University of Illinois at Chicago, 1984), 82.

32 Garfield Park Conservatory Alliance and LISC New Communities Program, *East Garfield Park: Growing A Healthy Community*, Quality of Life Plan, May, 2005.

33 Carol Kleiman, "Battling for the West Side" *Chicago Tribune*, November 2, 1980, F32.

34 Curtis Lawrence, "North Landale Garden is Firmly Rooted in Africa," *Chicago Sun-Tiimes*, July 2, 2001.

35 Neighborspace: Community Managed Open Space, www.neighbor-space.org/pg_african_heritage.htm.

36 Jens Jensen, *A Greater West Park System* (Chicago: West Chicago Park Commissioners, 1917), 14.

Photography Credits

Key

Brook Collins, Photojournalist,
Chicago Park District—BC
Chicago History Museum—CHM
Chicago Park District Special
Collections—CPD
Chicago Public Library Special
Collections and Preservation
Division—CPL
Chicago Transit Authority
Collection—CTA
Morton Arboretum Special
Collections—MA
Left—L
Right—R
Center—C
Top—T
Bottom—B

Front Cover: CPD
Flap, Back Cover, iv–1: BC.
2: CPD.
4: CHM, ICHi-51151.
5: CHM, ICHi-51150.
6 L: CPD, *Third Annual Report of the West Chicago Park Commissioners*, 1872.
   R: CPD.
8: CPD.
9 L: CHM, ICHi-51152.
   R: CPD, Third Annual Report of the West Chicago Park Commissioners, 1872.
10 L: CPD, *Sixth Annual Report West Chicago Park Commissioners*, 1875.
   R: CPD, *Sixth Annual Report West Chicago Park Commissioners*, 1875.
11: CPD, *Nineteenth Annual Report West Chicago Park Commissioners*, 1888.
12 L: CPD, *Twenty-Ninth Annual Report West Chicago Park Commissioners*, 1897.
   R: CPD, *Twenty-Eighth Annual Report West Chicago Park Commissioners*, 1896.
13 L: CHM, SDN-003386.
   R: CPD, *Twentieth Annual Report West Chicago Park Commissioners*, 1889.
14: CPD.
15: MA.
16: CPD, *Thirty-First Annual Report West Chicago Park Commissioners*, 1899.
17: CHM, ICHi-36405.
18–22: CPD.
23–24: CPD, *Forty-Seventh Annual Report West Chicago Park Commissioners*, 1915.
25: CPD, *A Greater West Park System*, 1920.
26: CPD.
27 TL: CHM, DN-0087346.
   TR: CHM, DN-0087344.
   B: CHM, SDN-068233.

28–39: CPD.
40–54: BC.
56: CHM, ICHi-17002.
58: www.mytimemachine.co.uk, *Dickinson's Comprehensive Pictures of the Great Exhibition of 1851*, 1854.
59: Special Collection and Archives Department, University Library, University of Massachusetts at Amherst.
60: CPD, *Twenty-Ninth Annual Report West Chicago Park Commissioners*, 1897.
61: CPD.
62: CPD, *Thirty-Ninth Annual Report West Chicago Park Commissioners*, 1907.
63–64: CPD.
65 L: MA.
   R: CPD
66 T: CPD.
   B: MA.
67: CPD.
68: MA.
69: CPD.
70 L: CPD.
   R: CPD, *Thirty-Eighth Annual Report West Chicago Park Commissioners*, 1906.
71: CPD.
72 L: CPD, "August Koch, Leader in Horticulture," *Parks & Recreation*, v.XXIV, n.4, 1940.
   R: CPD, *Catalog Guide to the Garfield Park Conservatory*, 1924.
73: CPD.
74: CHM, DN-0064334.
75: CHM, DN-0087772.
76–87: CPD.
88–90: BC.
91 L: CPD.
   R: BC.
92–102: BC.
104: CHM, ICHi-51168.

106 T: CHM, ICHi-30442.
   BL: ICHi-26325
   BR: CPD, *Twenty-Eighth Annual Report West Chicago Park Commissioners*, 1896.
108: CPD, *History of Chicago from the Earliest Period to the Present Time in Three Volumes*, A.T. Andreas, 1884.
110 L: CHM, SDN-003792.
   R: CHM, SDN-003706.
111 L,C: CTA, RT Routes-Lake St.
   R: CTA, RT Routes-Lake St.
112 L: CHM-DN-0002057.
   R: CPD.
113 L: Courtesy of Bill Latoza, Bauer Latoza Studio, Chicago.
   R: CPD.
114 T: CHM, ICHi-19155.
   BL: CPL, BNL 1.11.
   BR: CPL, BNL 2.5.
117: CPD.
118 L: CHM, ICHi-51166.
   R: CHM, ICHi-30442.
119 L: CHM, ICHi-20237.
   R: CHM, ICHi-23425.
120: CPL, BNL 9.1.
121 L: Courtesy of Mrs. Barbara Griffin.
   R: CHM, ICHi-51186.
123: CHM, ICHi-16958.
124 L: CHM, ICHi-26692A.
   R: CHM, ICHi-51183.
125: CHM, ICHi-51185.
126 L: CTA, Congress & Kedzie.
   R: CTA, Expressways: Congress (Eisenhower) Traffic.
127: CPL, BNL 12.21.
128: CPL, BNL 4.4.
129: CHM, ICHi-40016.
130 L: CHM, ICHi-51167.
   R: CHM, ICHi-51146.
131–140: BC.